MISSION
IN THE WAY
OF DANIEL

Endorsements

Mission in the Way of Daniel draws insights from biblical and historical theology as a model for contemporary mission in the public square. From the life of Daniel, Smither shows how God uses grief (exile and suffering) and gifting (natural ability and divine power) to carry his message to the nations. Many (rightly) highlight Daniel's faithful service, but the purpose of his suffering and service to exalt the supremacy of his God is often overlooked. Smither challenges us to consider how God wants to use the anguish and abilities in our lives to further his witness.

Brian Gault, PhD
Assistant Professor of Old Testament, Dallas Theological Seminary

This is a groundbreaking work of missional hermeneutics that offers thought-provoking assessments of the life, witness, and work of Daniel in the Hebrew Scriptures. Particularly striking is the scholarly integration of biblical theology of mission with a historical analysis of missions that speaks to our contemporary world.

Robert Gallagher, PhD
Emeritus Professor of Intercultural Studies, Wheaton College

Smither takes the reader on a fascinating and insightful journey, beginning with the life and book of Daniel, and making stops along the way in Scripture, mission history, and the contemporary world, demonstrating how the qualities that Daniel possessed and exercised are essential qualities for fulfilling today's mission as well. I heartily recommend this book for Christians who already have a passion for missions as well as for those who are seeking to be more relevant and fruitful in God's mission to transform their neighbors and the nations for his glory.

João Mordomo, PhD
Catalyst for Business as Mission, Lausanne Global Network

MISSION IN THE WAY OF DANIEL

Empowering Believers to Live into God's Plan

Edward L. Smither

Available at missionbooks.org

Mission in the Way of Daniel: Empowering Believers to Live into God's Plan

© 2022 by Edward L. Smither. All rights reserved.

No part of this book may be reproduced, stored in a retrieval system, or transmitted in any form or by any means—electronic, mechanical, photocopy, recording, or otherwise—without prior written permission from the publisher, except brief quotations used in connection with reviews in magazines or newspapers. For permission, email permissions@wclbooks.com. For corrections, email editor@wclbooks.com.

All Scripture quotations, unless otherwise indicated, are taken from the Holy Bible, New International Version®, NIV®. Copyright ©1973, 1978, 1984, 2011 by Biblica, Inc.™ Used by permission of Zondervan. All rights reserved worldwide. www.zondervan.com. The "NIV" and "New International Version" are trademarks registered in the United States Patent and Trademark Office by Biblica, Inc.™

Scripture quotations marked ESV are taken from the *ESV® Bible (The Holy Bible, English Standard Version®),* Copyright © 2001 by Crossway, a publishing ministry of Good News Publishers. Used by permission. All rights reserved.

Published by William Carey Publishing
10 W. Dry Creek Cir
Littleton, CO 80120 | www.missionbooks.org

William Carey Publishing is a ministry of Frontier Ventures
Pasadena, CA | www.frontierventures.org

Cover and Interior Designer: Mike Riester

ISBNs: 978-1-64508-420-4 (paperback)
 978-1-64508-422-8 (epub)

Printed Worldwide

26 25 24 23 22   1 2 3 4 5   IN

Library of Congress Control Number: 2022943795

Contents

Introduction	ix
Chapter 1: Vulnerable: Displaced for God's Mission	1
Chapter 2: Gifted: Natural Abilities for God's Mission	15
Chapter 3: Favored: God-Given Favor before Authorities	31
Chapter 4: Empowered: Experiencing and Demonstrating the Power of God in Mission	47
Chapter 5: Emboldened: Witness, Prayer, and Suffering	71
Appendix: Daniel: Background and Context	91
Acknowledgments	95
Bibliography	96
Scripture Index	101
Topical Index	104

Introduction

Loving our neighbors has never felt more complicated. Perhaps because the twenty-first-century world is a complicated place. A brief scroll through our social-media feeds reveals incredible polarization and hostility about politics, race, ethnicity, and gender identity. And a high percentage of our social-media content is simply misinformation and propaganda, making it hard to get a good read on what is actually true.

Our global family also faces significant crises in the areas of public health, civil war, terrorism, political and corporate corruption, poverty, and migration, among others. Amid such confusion and overwhelming problems, how can followers of Christ serve as viable witnesses to our neighbors, coworkers, and family members? How can we make disciples of all peoples in our day?

Several years ago, I gave a series of chapel messages at a Christian university on mission in a mobile world—our fast-paced, digitized, globalized, diaspora, and increasingly secular reality. I chose to develop my messages around the life and ministry of the Old Testament prophet Daniel. Preaching that week to the students (but mostly to myself), I became increasingly convinced that Daniel could offer us wisdom on serving Christ in mission in our current world.

Daniel was a cross-cultural missionary. When we think about missionary activity in Scripture, we're likely to envision the earthly ministry of Jesus, Paul's missionary journeys, and the witness of the early church in Acts before we think of Daniel. However, I define mission as *crossing boundaries between the people of God and the not yet people of God*. While we cross cultural boundaries in mission, declaring God's "glory among the nations" (Ps 96:3), the greatest barriers we cross in making disciples of all peoples (Matt 28:18–20) are faith barriers. Daniel lived, worked, and witnessed in a context in which people did not worship the one true God. Of course, culturally and religiously speaking, Daniel was a displaced Israelite who lived outside of his home culture, dwelling among the Babylonians and Persians.

Daniel was a displaced person, with significant natural and professional skills, who was bold in prayer and witness. Though his boldness resulted in suffering, he consistently found God-given favor with political leaders, and he experienced and demonstrated God's power in his witness. In this book, I unpack these qualities of Daniel's mission that are observable within the book of Daniel. I then explore them further in other parts of Scripture, in mission history, and in the contemporary world. Then I argue for why each quality is a necessary component of mission today.

Perhaps now more than ever, Daniel's model for witness is needed in the twenty-first-century context. Daniel's firsthand account as a displaced person speaks to the more than eighty million internally and externally displaced people in the world today.[1] In many parts of the world, traditional religious workers (pastors and missionaries) are discredited because of scandals or perceptions of the clergy from the media, movies, and TV. In other places, such as the Muslim world and China, professional clergy are not allowed and have no place in society. So the model of a professional worker, living with integrity and witnessing as a way of life in the marketplace and public square, is meaningful.[2] In a world in which people are skeptical of religion and religious people, Christians following Daniel's model can provide a refreshing testimony for Christ.

> *Perhaps now more than ever, Daniel's model for witness is needed in the twenty-first-century context.*

Finally, many nonbelievers in the world are concerned with maintaining power and control over their own lives. How will they pass exams, find a spouse, have healthy children, land a job, or ensure their spouse will remain faithful? For those who feel powerless, Daniel witnesses to a God of strength, power, and presence.

In the appendix at the end, I provide a brief context for the narrative chapters of the book of Daniel. If you need that context, read that first. If not, continue to chapters 1 to 5, where I unpack each of the characteristics of Daniel on mission:

1. Daniel was a displaced believer who serves from a posture of vulnerability.
2. He was gifted with natural and professional skills.
3. He gained favor with political leaders.

---

1 See "Figures at a Glance." Displaced persons who remain in their home country are considered internally displaced, while those who leave their country are considered externally displaced, refugees, or asylum seekers.

2 See further Fernando, *Spiritual Living*, 14–15.

4. He experienced and demonstrated God's power in mission.
5. He boldly witnessed about God while suffering.

At the end of each chapter, I provide some questions for reflection. For groups reading through this book together, these questions will provide rich opportunities for discussion and application, especially as we reflect on mission in the way of Daniel for today.

I am writing this book for believers in Christ who already have a heart for mission—those who care about engaging our world in Christian mission for this present day. This includes pastors, missionaries, and other full-time Christian workers, but I'm especially writing for those called to the marketplace to be excellent employees and available witnesses for Christ. I think students of biblical and mission studies striving to craft a theology of mission will also benefit from this book.

Though this is not a work of biblical scholarship per se, I do build on the work of Daniel scholars to support my claims. I read the book of Daniel (as I read all of Scripture) with a hermeneutic of mission. Since the mission of God is a grand theme throughout all of Scripture, I approach Daniel within that framework.[3] This assumption supports my methodology of analyzing mission principles in Daniel, discussing them within the broader canonical Scriptures, and then exploring them through church and mission history.

I am motivated to offer this study because I think Daniel can be overlooked in mission studies, and because Daniel's life, work, and witness speak to our times.

---

3 See further Wright, *Mission of God*, 29–74; also Goheen, ed., *Reading the Bible Missionally*.

CHAPTER 1

Vulnerable: Displaced for God's Mission

In the opening of his book, Daniel wastes no time recounting how his homeland was conquered by the Babylonian king, Nebuchadnezzar, and how he and three friends were taken into captivity and exiled to Babylon.

> *In the third year of the reign of Jehoiakim king of Judah, Nebuchadnezzar king of Babylon came to Jerusalem and besieged it. And the Lord delivered Jehoiakim king of Judah into his hand, along with some of the articles from the temple of God. These he carried off to the temple of his god in Babylonia and put in the treasure house of his god.*
>
> *Then the king ordered Ashpenaz, chief of his court officials, to bring into the king's service some of the Israelites from the royal family and the nobility— young men without any physical defect, handsome, showing aptitude for every kind of learning, well informed, quick to understand, and qualified to serve in the king's palace. He was to teach them the language and literature of the Babylonians. The king assigned them a daily amount of food and wine from*

> *the king's table. They were to be trained for three years, and after that they were to enter the king's service.*
>
> *Among those who were chosen were some from Judah: Daniel, Hananiah, Mishael and Azariah. The chief official gave them new names: to Daniel, the name Belteshazzar; to Hananiah, Shadrach; to Mishael, Meshach; and to Azariah, Abednego. ...*
>
> *And Daniel remained there until the first year of King Cyrus.* (Dan 1:1–7, 21)

In the first of three deportations of the Israelites,[1] the Babylonians took members of the royal family and the nobility. An intentional move, the Babylonians wanted to cripple any Israelite leadership by creating dependency on the Babylonian court. By exiling Daniel and other noble youth, they were also weakening the prospects of future leadership in Judah.[2]

Daniel and his friends were taken when they were only teenagers. Daniel would ultimately spend seventy years of his life in exile. Though he would have witnessed the first Jewish exiles' return to Jerusalem under the Persian King Cyrus, Daniel probably never saw his homeland again.[3]

In addition to removing the young men from their homeland, the Babylonians changed their names. This not only robbed them of their personal and cultural identities, but since their names had religious significance, it was also an attempt to diminish their Jewish faith. The Hebrew name Daniel means "God is my judge"; Hananiah means "The LORD shows grace"; Mishael means "Who is what God is?"; and Azariah means "The LORD helps." Their new names—Belteshazzar (Daniel's new name), Shadrach, Meshach, and Abednego—also had religious meanings—only now, they paid homage to the Babylonian deities.[4]

Though Daniel and his friends would find favor and be promoted in Babylon and Persia and spend the remainder of their days there, they would still be regarded as foreigners. Throughout the narrative, the Babylonians and Persians identify them as "exiles from Judah" (Dan 2:25;

---

1 These occurred in 605, 597, and 586 BC. During the third wave, Jerusalem completely fell to the Babylonians.

2 See further Goldingay, *Daniel*, 15; Longman, *Daniel*, 47; and Duguid and Wegner, "Daniel: Introduction and Notes," 1586.

3 See further Archer and Youngblood, "Daniel: Introduction and Notes," 1464; also Longman, *Daniel*, 18.

4 See further Longman, *Daniel*, 51; and Goldingay, *Daniel*, 24.

5:13; 6:13). While Daniel and his friends come to understand the language, culture, literature, and political workings of their host people, they never fully assimilate because of their faith in the God of Israel. When certain Babylonian court officials denounce Shadrach, Meshach, and Abednego to Nebuchadnezzar, they refer to them as "some Jews whom you have set over the affairs of the province of Babylon ... who pay no attention to you. ... They neither serve your gods nor worship the image of gold you have set up" (Dan 3:12).

Migration in Scripture

Daniel's story of displacement is not unusual. The Bible contains many accounts of migration and peoples on the move. Christopher Wright argues that "Migration runs like a thread through the whole Bible narrative. People on the move are so much a part of the fabric of the story we hardly notice it as a major feature."[5]

In sketching out a theology of migration, Andrew Walls classifies two types of migration in Scripture—Adamic and Abrahamic.[6] Describing the first, Walls writes:

> *In the story of Adam and Eve we meet involuntary migration, migration that stands for loss: loss of home, loss of well-being, loss of expectations; migration that represents a transition from a desirable to a far less desirable way of life.*[7]

Because of their ingratitude and disobedience, the first couple is forcibly removed from the garden (Gen 3:4–19). So Adamic migration is "punitive" and "the result of wrongdoing."[8] In Genesis, this migration continues after Cain murders his brother (Gen 4:13–16) and is "condemned to a wandering life of continual migration, away from the kinship group whose bonds he has violated."[9]

We observe it again when the gathered nations construct the Tower of Babel, a symbol of their pride and refusal to obey the cultural mandate to "be fruitful and increase in number, fill the earth and subdue it" (Gen 1:28). God destroys the tower, confuses their languages, and disperses

---
5 Wright, "Shared Human Condition," 144.
6 Walls, "Toward a Theology of Migration," 51–57.
7 Walls, 52.
8 Walls, 53.
9 Walls, 52–53.

the peoples (Gen 11:1–9).[10] Ironically, God, in judgment, pushes the nations out to *fulfill* the cultural mandate.

Contrasting Adam's plight and Abraham's migration, Walls writes, "Abraham leaves in hope, with the expectation of a better life. ... The stimulus to leave ... is the divine call, the initiative of God. ... Abraham's migration has a missionary aspect."[11] This hopeful pilgrimage can also be observed in the lives of Isaac and Jacob (Gen 26:2–5; 32:22–32). For Walls, Abrahamic migration continues with the Exodus, when God delivers his people from slavery in Egypt and leads them to a place of flourishing in the Promised Land.[12] It is also the basis for the missionary movements of the Apostle Paul and the early church, making disciples of all peoples and taking the gospel to the ends of the earth.

> *Though Abrahamic migrants are virtuous people who sojourn in hope, they are not spared hardship along the way.*

Though Abrahamic migrants are virtuous people who sojourn in hope, they are not spared hardship along the way. Their initial migration could be provoked by the evil actions of others. Though Joseph's presence in Egypt brought blessing to the family of Jacob and was the seed for the Exodus centuries later, Joseph initially moves to Egypt involuntarily because of the jealous and violent actions of his brothers (Gen 37:18–36). Mary and Joseph and the infant Jesus seek refuge in Egypt before returning to Nazareth because of Herod's murderous campaign against baby boys (Matt 2:13–18).

Finally, while the early church is called to be Christ's "witnesses in Jerusalem, and in all Judea and Samaria, and to the ends of the earth" (Acts 1:8), the latter part of the call is fulfilled in part because "a great persecution broke out against the church in Jerusalem, and all except the apostles were scattered throughout Judea and Samaria" (Acts 8:1).

As I read Wall's categories of biblical migration, I think there might also be a third category: Abrahamic migration *within* Adamic migration. That is, within a group that is exiled for their sin and disobedience, there

---

10 See further Walls, 53.

11 Walls, 53–54.

12 See further Walls, 54–55.

are righteous people—a remnant—who serve the Lord in a redemptive manner. This is how I see the story of Daniel and his friends.

After a long history of disobedience, Israel was conquered and exiled, first by the Assyrians and then by the Babylonians. While tragic, this came as no surprise, since God had repeatedly reminded his chosen ones that failing to keep the covenant would result in judgment. In Deuteronomy 4:27, God promises: "The LORD will scatter you among the peoples, and only a few of you will survive among the nations to which the LORD will drive you."[13] Though Nebuchadnezzar conquers Judah and plunders the temple (his attempt to show his greatness and the greatness of his gods over the God of Israel), Daniel is clear that "*the Lord* delivered Jehoiakim king of Judah into his [Nebuchanezzar's] hand" (Dan 1:2; emphasis mine).[14] Longman notes that Daniel calls God "the Lord" (*Adonai*), which refers to his "ownership" and "control" of the situation. In allowing the temple to be plundered and Jerusalem to fall, God makes good on his covenant promises and shows his sovereignty.[15]

> *Within a group that is exiled for their sin and disobedience, there are righteous people—a remnant—who serve the Lord in a redemptive manner. This is how I see the story of Daniel and his friends.*

Daniel and his friends suffered the hardships of displacement through no apparent fault of their own. In this sense, John Goldingay argues for a parallel connection between Daniel's experience and Joseph's involuntary migration to Egypt, which came at the hands of his wicked brothers.[16] Though Daniel certainly felt the injustice against himself, he also identifies with sinful Israel and Judah in a corporate prayer of repentance:

---

13 See also Lev 26:14–46 and Deut 28:64.
14 See further Goldingay, *Daniel*, 15, 21; see also Dan 9:11–14.
15 See further Longman, *Daniel*, 46; also Duguid and Wegner, "Daniel: Introduction and Notes," 1586; and Fewell, *Circle of Sovereignty*, 14–15.
16 See further Goldingay, *Daniel*, 16.

> *I prayed to the Lord my God and confessed:*
>
> *"Lord, the great and awesome God, who keeps his covenant of love with those who love him and keep his commandments, we have sinned and done wrong. We have been wicked and have rebelled; we have turned away from your commands and laws. We have not listened to your servants the prophets, who spoke in your name to our kings, our princes and our ancestors, and to all the people of the land.*
>
> *Lord, you are righteous, but this day we are covered with shame—the people of Judah and the inhabitants of Jerusalem and all Israel, both near and far, in all the countries where you have scattered us because of our unfaithfulness to you. We and our kings, our princes and our ancestors are covered with shame, Lord, because we have sinned against you. The Lord our God is merciful and forgiving, even though we have rebelled against him; we have not obeyed the Lord our God or kept the laws he gave us through his servants the prophets. All Israel has transgressed your law and turned away, refusing to obey you." (Daniel 9:4–11)*

Goldingay adds that exile did not signify the end of God's work for Israel and Judah. He writes that they "are still within the sphere of his activity, even though it does not look like it. ... To be in the hand of Nebuchadnezzar is not to be out of the control of God."[17] While the temple articles were taken to Babylon, more importantly, a faithful worshiping remnant (Daniel and friends and others) also went and were used by God to bless the exiled people of God.[18]

Migration in the Mission of God

Within the migration theme that runs through Scripture, we also observe that God scatters and gathers. That is, while dispersing sinful peoples in his judgment, God demonstrates his mercy by allowing exiled, dispersed strangers and foreigners to return home or to migrate to a new place of flourishing. In the Genesis narrative, immediately following the destruction of the Tower of Babel and the dispersion of the nations, the Lord sets Abraham apart for a redemptive purpose:

---

17 Goldingay, *Daniel*, 22.
18 See further Goldingay, 22; also Fewell, *Circle of Sovereignty*, 15.

> *The Lord had said to Abram, "Go from your country, your people and your father's household to the land I will show you.*
>
> > *"I will make you into a great nation,*
> > > *and I will bless you;*
> > *I will make your name great,*
> > > *and you will be a blessing.*
> > *I will bless those who bless you,*
> > > *and whoever curses you I will curse;*
> > *and all peoples on earth*
> > > *will be blessed through you." (Gen 12:1–3)*

Abraham was set apart and blessed by God so that through his offspring, ultimately the Messiah, the gospel would go to all peoples, including those scattered by divine judgement. Paul puts it this way: "Scripture foresaw that God would justify the Gentiles by faith, and announced the gospel in advance to Abraham: All nations will be blessed through you'" (Gal 3:8). The problems that emerge from Babel in Genesis 11 are answered by the plan of a merciful God in Genesis 12.[19]

God's blessing through Abraham can also be observed on the Day of Pentecost. "God-fearing Jews from every nation under heaven" (Acts 2:5) had traveled to Jerusalem for the feast. When the Holy Spirit came upon the apostles, they spoke in tongues, communicating the gospel in power. Luke, the author of Acts, continues,

> *When they [God-fearing Jews] heard this sound, a crowd came together in bewilderment, because each one heard their own language being spoken. Utterly amazed, they asked: "Aren't all these who are speaking Galileans? Then how is it that each of us hears them in our native language? Parthians, Medes and Elamites; residents of Mesopotamia, Judea and Cappadocia, Pontus and Asia, Phrygia and Pamphylia, Egypt and the parts of Libya near Cyrene; visitors from Rome (both Jews and converts to Judaism); Cretans and Arabs—we hear them declaring the wonders of God in our own tongues!" (Acts 2:6–11)*

In what would amount to a reversal of Babel, God is pleased to gather this diverse group of Jews together to hear and believe the gospel. After the Spirit moves, Peter preaches, and "Those who accepted his

---
19 See further Deut 32:8–9.

message were baptized, and about three thousand were added to their number that day" (Acts 2:41).

God also takes scattered people and makes them a blessing to other strangers and foreigners in their midst.[20] Since the people of Israel had been "foreigners in Egypt," they were commanded to "not mistreat or oppress a foreigner" (Exod 22:21). Similarly, Leviticus 19:33–34 contains this statute: "When a foreigner resides among you in your land, do not mistreat them. The foreigner residing among you must be treated as your native-born. Love them as yourself, for you were foreigners in Egypt."

God called Israel to show hospitality to strangers by providing food, treating foreigners fairly in court, offering fair work wages, and including them in Israel's religious festivals, such as the Sabbath, the Day of Atonement, and the Passover. Essentially, foreigners were to be treated as if they were citizens of Israel.[21] This inclusion in Israel's worship life implies that many foreigners became believers in Israel's God. In obeying these laws, Boaz welcomed the Moabite widow, Ruth, into his field before marrying her (Ruth 2:1–4:13). Ruth also became a believer in Israel's God (Ruth 1:16).[22]

Finally, God seems pleased to use those who are displaced to be his witnesses. As we will see, Daniel not only ministered to his own people in exile, but he also proclaimed God's ways to the Babylonians and Persians. Though Daniel does receive favor and promotions within these governments, he never escapes being viewed as a foreigner and serving from a posture of vulnerability.

> *God seems pleased to use those who are displaced to be his witnesses.*

Looking back to Genesis, we have noted a similar pattern in the life and service of Joseph in Egypt. Looking to the New Testament, we see further evidence of this, for example, in the opening address of Peter's first letter:

---

20 Wright ("A Shared Human Condition," 146–47) distinguishes between the types of foreigners in the Old Testament—*gerim* ("resident alien" or "immigrant") and *nokryim* and *zarim* (complete outsiders to Israel and those who worship other gods). Here we are discussing Israel's relationship to the *gerim*.

21 See further Jipp, *Saved by Faith and Hospitality*, 141; also Exod 12:48–49; Deut 1:16–17; 5:14–15; 16:11–14; 24:14–22; 31:9–13; Lev 16:29; 19:9–10; 23:22; 24:22; Num 9:14; 15:15–16.

22 See further Smither, *Mission as Hospitality*, 21–25.

> To God's elect, exiles scattered throughout the provinces of Pontus, Galatia, Cappadocia, Asia and Bithynia, who have been chosen according to the foreknowledge of God the Father, through the sanctifying work of the Spirit, to be obedient to Jesus Christ and sprinkled with his blood. (1 Pet 1:1–2)

Though they are scattered and vulnerable, Peter exhorts them to "Live such good lives among the pagans that, though they accuse you of doing wrong, they may see your good deeds and glorify God on the day he visits us" (1 Pet 2:12).

Migration and Mission in History

While the mission of God in history has been accomplished by some who have voluntarily gone to the nations in faith, hope, and obedience, others have found themselves in unplanned cross-cultural settings. When I think about Daniel being forcibly displaced to Babylon in his teens, I am reminded of another teenager, Patrick of Ireland (ca. 389 to ca. 461), whose abduction eventually led to the evangelization of Ireland.

Patrick was born in Western Roman Britain to a wealthy, noble, and believing family. Patrick's father served as a deacon in the church, while his grandfather was a priest. At the age of sixteen, Patrick experienced a radical reversal when he was captured and enslaved by a band of Irish invaders. He ended up spending six years in slavery.

Though raised in a Christian family, Patrick had resisted surrendering his life to Christ. However, during his time in captivity, amid long days tending sheep, he began to pray, eventually embracing the gospel for himself. In addition to this spiritual formation, Patrick was learning the language, culture, and religious worldview of the Irish—training that would help him later as a missionary.

After six years in captivity, Patrick had a vision directing him to escape, board a ship, and return home. After some time back with his family, Patrick received a new vision. This time it was the voice of the Irish calling him back to live among them. Though his family were Christians, they found it unthinkable that he would return to the people who had enslaved him. Reflecting on these visions later in life, Patrick wrote: "The one and only purpose I had in going back to the people from whom I had earlier escaped was the gospel and the promises of God."[23]

---

23 Patrick, *Confessions*, 61, in O'Loughlin, *St. Patrick*.

After apprenticing in ministry under a bishop in either Gaul or Britain, Patrick was set apart by Bishop Celestine of Rome as a missionary bishop to the Irish. Believing he was living in the last days and serving at the ends of the earth, Patrick was motivated to make disciples of the Irish (Matt 24:14; 28:18–20). Since Ireland was a lawless place in the fifth century, hardship and danger regularly stalked his path.

In his mission practice, Patrick would first approach tribal elders, announce his missionary intentions, and seek the leaders' favor. From there, he engaged in itinerant preaching and would catechize, or teach, those who had received the gospel. Church planting naturally followed, and Patrick probably started as many as two hundred new churches in Ireland. Along with the churches, he established a network of monasteries, which provided a means for spiritual formation and a structure for a church network.

By the time he died, Patrick had led some one hundred thousand Irish to faith in Christ. But his impact didn't stop at the shores of this small island. In the generations that followed, the Irish church became the leading missionary movement in the evangelization of Europe.[24]

When we evaluate Patrick's story in light of Walls' theology of migration categories, his story follows the Abrahamic pattern. Like Joseph and Daniel, Patrick was forcibly displaced against his will; however, God sovereignly used Patrick's sojourn in slavery to bring him to faith in Christ. Following later visions, Patrick willfully returned to Ireland to preach the gospel.

Migration and Mission in the Modern World

We live in an increasingly globalized world. I define globalization as the interconnectivity of our world in the realms of business, government, and interpersonal relationships.[25] As Harvard business professor Rosabeth Moss Kantor describes it, "The world is becoming a global shopping mall in which ideas and products are available everywhere at the same time."[26] Because of increased global business, affordable travel, and technology (especially the internet and social media), the world has become much smaller.[27]

---

24 See further Smither, *Missionary Monks*, 51–63.
25 See further Steger, *Globalization*, 3.
26 Cited in Myers, *Engaging Globalization*, 34.
27 See further Myers, 33–144.

Global migration contributes significantly to the phenomenon of globalization. However, the mention of migration or immigration often engenders fearful and angry responses, particularly during political campaigns in the Western world. Some candidates stoke these fears by conflating all forms of immigration into the category of illegal immigration.

In order to address these fears and the ignorance that drives them, it is important to clarify the various ways in which people migrate in our current world. I would describe a first group as willful and even *privileged immigrants*. These include professionals—entrepreneurs, CEOs, engineers, IT specialists, university professors and researchers—who migrate to advance their career ambitions. Many of these begin as international students, those who receive scholarships from their home governments or host universities or simply possess personal wealth to be able to pursue their educational goals. According to the most recent data available, about 1.1 million international students are studying in the United States.[28]

In a second group, we have *global laborers*. They have migrated for work because of limited employment opportunities in their home country and are motivated by survival. A good example of this group are the millions of Filipinos who migrate every year to work as domestic help in the oil-rich Gulf countries or in factories in Canada. Historically, such guest workers seek work in the nation that colonized theirs. For example, millions of North Africans migrated to France to work in factories during the twentieth century. Though Morocco, Algeria, and Tunisia had all gained independence from France by 1962, many laborers remained in France because of greater opportunities for work.

In the final group, we have those who have migrated because of *forced displacement*. Because of war, political tyranny, famine, or other atrocities, they have fled their homes and cities and sought refuge in a safer environment. Those who have done that within the borders of their home country are considered internally displaced, while those who cross national borders to seek refuge are called externally displaced, or refugees. Those who have fled specifically due to political tyranny or religious persecution are deemed asylum seekers. Europe classifies all refugees as asylum seekers.[29]

Those born and raised in the Western world might be surprised by the sheer pervasiveness of displaced people. By 2021, over 82 million

---

28 Israel and Batalova, "International Students in the United States."
29 See further International Association for Refugees.

people (one out of ninety-five people in the world) had been forcibly displaced. This was an increase from 40 million in 2009. Women and girls make up half of the world's displaced population. Forty-one percent are children. About 26 million of the world's forcibly displaced people would be considered refugees.

Most of the refugees in the world come from Syria, Palestine, Venezuela, Afghanistan, South Sudan, Myanmar, Democratic Republic of Congo, Somalia, Sudan, and Central African Republic. Though Europe is the most desired destination on the refugee highway, around 86 percent of refugees actually reside in developing countries. Turkey, Colombia, Pakistan, Uganda, and Germany (the only developed nation on this list) are the top refugee-receiving nations in the world. Nearly one-sixth of Lebanon's population is comprised of refugees from Palestine and Syria.[30]

The reality of migration in the present world has challenged the church to reconsider how we think about and approach Christian mission. Mission thinkers have embraced a field of study called diaspora missiology—"a missiological framework for understanding and participating in God's redemptive mission among people living outside their place of origin."[31] For example, we recognize that the direction and flow of mission has become polycentric, "from everyone to everyone."[32] We also recognize that as people migrate, they negotiate new cultural identities. Algerian youth who've grown up in France (many of whom prefer to speak French over Arabic) are culturally different from their extended family in North Africa.

In a globalized and diaspora world, mission has shifted in some respects from going to the nations to welcoming the nations. Many churches in the West have embraced ministering to international professionals in their communities. Some mission organizations have launched with the purpose of welcoming international students—offering welcoming friendship, demonstrating hospitality, and conducting seeker Bible studies, among other services.[33] An increasing number of groups are ministering to refugees in word (sharing Christ) and deed (caring for tangible needs). In these efforts, missionaries and volunteers teach English, assist with job placement, encourage small-business development, help with medical issues, and care for those who have faced mental and emotional trauma.

---

30 See further "The Refugee Highway."
31 "The Seoul Declaration on Diaspora Missiology."
32 See further Yeh, *Polycentric Missiology*.
33 See further EveryInternational.

Some organizations assist asylum seekers who are walking through the legal and administrative steps.[34]

Like Daniel, sometimes people on the move become the missionaries themselves, bringing a witness for Christ to their adopted homeland.[35] International student Bible studies in North America are often led by other believing international students. At a recent national prayer breakfast in Washington, DC, the ambassador from Guatemala offered a powerful witness for Christ in his prayers for the American president. In the greater Toronto area, many new churches have been planted because of the presence of Filipino guest workers.

In some cases, refugees who are reached with the gospel begin to minister to others. I know a student from Syria who became a follower of Christ through the compassionate witness of aid workers in Turkey. As the student journeyed on the refugee highway through Europe, he vowed to be a witness for Christ to others on the way.

Summary: Toward Vulnerable Mission

> *Mission in the way of Daniel is a witness from a posture of vulnerability.*

In the book of Daniel, through the whole of Scripture, across the sweep of mission history, and even in the present day, the mission of God is accomplished in a diaspora world. It is accomplished among and by people on the move. As we consider the different types of immigrants in the present world (the externally displaced, migrating professionals, students, and workers), many of them can relate to Daniel's experience. He was privileged, educated, and had professional skills, which we will explore in the next chapter, but he was also displaced against his will. We might argue that Daniel is a composite immigrant, and his story resonates with the story of millions in our world today.

Though Daniel was an involuntary immigrant who probably faced hardship in his initial displacement, his migration does seem to follow the Abrahamic pattern. Daniel leaves the security of his homeland and is blessed to be a blessing among the nations in Babylon, Persia, and

---

34 See further Jonathan House, a ministry of International Association for Refugees, which provides shelter for asylum seekers in St. Paul, Minnesota, https://www.iafr.org/project/jonathan-house.

35 See further Hanciles, *Migration and the Making*, 1.

even beyond. A worshiper of the Most High God displaced among nonbelievers, Daniel becomes a diaspora missionary. It also seems that Daniel's witness to dispersed Jews comes full circle when their descendants ("Parthians, Medes and Elamites") journey up to Jerusalem at Pentecost and hear the good news in their own tongues through the power of the Holy Spirit (Acts 2:9).

Finally, mission in the way of Daniel is a witness from a posture of vulnerability. Displaced from his homeland and even stripped of his given name, Daniel had no authority in Babylon and Persia. Though he will find favor and be promoted, his witness does not flow from a place of power. Daniel's mission, along with the witness of many diaspora missionaries today, challenges the narrative of colonial or Christendom mission. In a context of polycentric mission, may all global Christians embrace weakness and vulnerability on the road to making disciples of all peoples.[36]

Questions for Reflection

1. Thinking about Daniel as an involuntary immigrant who witnessed for the Lord in a foreign court, consider how that concept challenges our paradigm for what a missionary is today. How might immigrants, and even refugees, be fruitful missionaries?

2. How might scattered peoples today (both believers and nonbelievers) find hope in Daniel's story?

3. Daniel exemplified mission from a place of weakness, or vulnerability. How does his example challenge notions we have of mission work or missionaries today?

4. After reading this chapter, what is one step of faith you can take in your walk of faith this week?

---

36 See further Harries, *Vulnerable Mission*; also Flanders, "Vulnerable Mission."

CHAPTER 2

Gifted: Natural Abilities for God's Mission

Even a cursory reading of the book of Daniel reveals that Daniel and his companions were renaissance men. God endowed them with significant natural abilities—skills to be used for his glory among the nations in Babylon, Persia, and beyond. Embedded in the narrative of the opening chapter of Daniel is an impressive resume of qualities:

> Then the king ordered Ashpenaz, chief of his court officials, to bring into the king's service some of the Israelites from the royal family and the nobility—young men without any physical defect, handsome, showing aptitude for every kind of learning, well informed, quick to understand, and qualified to serve in the king's palace. He was to teach them the language and literature of the Babylonians. The king assigned them a daily amount of food and wine from the king's table. They were to be trained for three years, and after that they were to enter the king's service. ...

> *To these four young men God gave knowledge and understanding of all kinds of literature and learning. And Daniel could understand visions and dreams of all kinds.*
>
> *At the end of the time set by the king to bring them into his service, the chief official presented them to Nebuchadnezzar. The king talked with them, and he found none equal to Daniel, Hananiah, Mishael and Azariah; so they entered the king's service. In every matter of wisdom and understanding about which the king questioned them, he found them ten times better than all the magicians and enchanters in his whole kingdom. (Dan 1:3–5, 17–20)*

Physical Health

Daniel and his friends possessed strong, healthy bodies, and they were good-looking too. Not unlike the temple articles that were taken from Jerusalem, the young men were without physical defect. Some commentators make a connection between these young exiles and Absalom, King David's heir apparent (2 Sam 14:25).[1]

> *Their allegiance was to the God of Israel—the one true God.*

Daniel's good health was in part due to a diet of vegetables and water and an approved request to pass on the food served at the Babylonian king's table (Dan 1:8–16). A few explanations have been proposed for this request. First, Daniel may have been concerned about eating meat that had been sacrificed to idols. Though a valid point, it's possible that the vegetables he consumed could have also been dedicated to idols. Second, Daniel and friends may have refused the king's food because it would have made them ceremonially unclean—an affront to their convictions as pious Jews (Lev 11:1–47; Deut 14:3–20). Third, Daniel may have passed because the menu, particularly meat and wine, consisted of foods eaten at a celebration. Since their homeland was under siege and they were being forcibly displaced, perhaps they were in mourning and unable to stomach a celebration meal.

---

[1] See further Goldingay, *Daniel*, 23; Longman, *Daniel*, 49; and Duguid and Wegner, "Daniel: Introduction and Notes," 1586.

While these are good arguments, the most compelling explanation is that the young men wanted to distinguish themselves from the other Jewish exiles (who were eating the king's food) and reject any dependency on the Babylonian court for their survival. Their allegiance was to the God of Israel—the one true God.[2] Since they were set apart because of their faith convictions, they would demonstrate that by observing an austere diet. Through God's favor, their convictions, and their clean eating, they remained healthy and strong young men.[3]

Knowledge and Wisdom

Daniel and friends also possessed natural skills for knowledge and wisdom. The Babylonians recognized their potential, since they were "showing aptitude for every kind of learning, well informed, quick to understand, and qualified to serve in the king's palace" (Dan 1:4). Goldingay remarks that similar language was used to describe Kings David and Solomon, who were "learned, knowledgeable, and discerning."[4]

Given their recognized potential for learning, Daniel and friends entered a training program in which they studied "the language and literature of the Babylonians" (Dan 1:4). While Daniel learned Aramaic, the vernacular Babylonian language which he uses for Daniel 2:4b–7:28, his training in literature required a mastery of the classical languages of Sumerian and Akkadian.[5] Babylonian literature included works of history, mythology, hero stories, and poetry. Daniel, of course, studied the literature in order to become a Babylonian sage—a practitioner in religion, medicine, astronomy, astrology, and divination. As the narrative of Daniel shows, the Babylonian kings valued sages to make sense of phenomena (dreams, signs, omens) in the world.[6]

Though it may appear that Daniel was compromising his faith by practicing divination in the Babylonian context, the Bible does not condemn divination directly. Rather, it condemns pagan beliefs and practices that oppose worship of the one true God. At any rate, the

---

2 See further Fewell, *Circle of Sovereignty*, 16–21.

3 See further Goldingay, *Daniel*, 18–19; Fernando, *Spiritual Living*, 16–17; Archer and Youngblood, "Daniel: Introduction and Notes," 1463; and Duguid and Wegner, "Daniel: Introduction and Notes," 1586.

4 See further 1 Sam 16:12, 18; 18:5, 14–15; 1 Kgs 5:9–14; Goldingay, *Daniel*, 16, 23.

5 Since Aramaic was a lingua franca in the ancient world, it's possible that Daniel may have learned it before his displacement to Babylon.

6 See further Goldingay, *Daniel*, 16–17; also Longman, *Daniel*, 49–50.

God of Israel did not typically speak to his people through divination.[7] Studying the language, culture, and literature of the Babylonians provided Daniel with great insights into the Babylonian context that would help his witness. Ajith Fernando observes, "Studying the thought world of Gentiles was something the average devout Jew did not bother with." However, as displaced people seeking to live and worship God in a pagan context, Daniel and his friends' "knowledge of Babylonian thinking would have helped them a great deal in this witness."[8]

Because of God's blessing, Daniel and friends exceeded all expectations for knowledge and wisdom. Excelling at the divining arts of the Babylonians, Daniel "could understand visions and dreams of all kinds" (Dan 1:17).[9] Nebuchadnezzar found Daniel and friends to be "ten times better than all the magicians and enchanters in his whole kingdom" (Dan 1:20). Goldingay adds, "God, the true God of Israel, is the source of the young men's insight and of Daniel's achievements in the Babylonians' own area of expertise."[10] While God condemns Babylon for its magic and sorcery in Isaiah 47, he demonstrates his power over the Babylonians through the presence and work of Daniel.[11]

Leadership and Administration

Throughout the book, Daniel, Shadrach, Meshach, and Abednego are appointed to places of political leadership in Babylon and Persia. Because of God's favor, they are also promoted. After Daniel's success interpreting Nebuchadnezzar's dream, the king makes him "ruler over the entire province of Babylon and placed him in charge of all its wise men" (Dan 2:48). While the text does not specify what Daniel's duties are as ruler, we do know that he is placed in authority over all of his fellow sages.

We also learn that Daniel convinces the king to make Shadrach, Meshach, and Abednego "administrators over the province of Babylon" (Dan 2:49).[12] Following their miraculous survival of the fiery furnace, the men are "promoted ... in the province of Babylon" (Dan 3:30). After Daniel interprets the writing on the wall for Belshazzar, the king fulfills his promise and makes Daniel "the third highest ruler in the kingdom" (Dan 5:16, 29).

---

7 See further Goldingay, *Daniel*, 27.
8 Fernando, *Spiritual Living*, 21–22.
9 See further Longman, *Daniel*, 55–56.
10 Goldingay, *Daniel*, 27.
11 See further Goldingay, *Daniel*, 27.
12 See further Goldingay, 52.

That position was short-lived, however, since Darius the Mede "took over the kingdom" and killed Belshazzar "that very night" (Dan 5:30–31).

Though we would expect Daniel to find himself out of a job with the demise of the Babylonian Empire, he continues to have a place within the new Persian Empire. Daniel writes,

> *It pleased Darius to appoint 120 satraps to rule throughout the kingdom, with three administrators over them, one of whom was Daniel. The satraps were made accountable to them so that the king might not suffer loss. Now Daniel so distinguished himself among the administrators and the satraps by his exceptional qualities that the king planned to set him over the whole kingdom. (Dan 6:1–3)*

Within this administrative structure, satraps were "provincial rulers, responsible for security and collection of tribute."[13] As the text indicates, they were overseen by three administrators, or presidents—one of whom is Daniel. Because Daniel continued to excel, the king planned to promote him in the new government. This intended advancement fuels the jealousy of the other Persian administrators and satraps, and they conspire to discredit him, ultimately leading to Daniel being thrown in the lions' den.

Though we possess little detail about Daniel or his friends' actual work in their government posts, they must have been skilled leaders to not only remain in those positions but also to be promoted in them.[14] Daniel's leadership and administrative skills were valued by two different imperial administrations.

Daniel, Shadrach, Meshach, and Abednego were blessed by God with natural abilities that allowed them to have a place of influence for God in Babylon and Persia. All four were healthy, strong men who captured the attention of those in authority. Though never fully accepted as cultural insiders, they set themselves apart from both their Babylonian and Jewish colleagues through their attention to their studies. Because of Daniel's skills in dream interpretation, he became a leader among the Babylonian sages. In addition to their God-given wisdom, the four Israelites were skilled leaders and administrators who could concretely "seek the peace and prosperity of the city" where they lived in exile (Jer 29:7).[15]

---

13 Duguid and Wegner, "Daniel: Introduction and Notes," 1597; see also Goldingay, *Daniel*, 127.

14 See further Goldingay, *Daniel*, 123.

15 See further Duguid and Wegner, "Daniel: Introduction and Notes," 1590–91.

Natural Abilities for Mission in Scripture

Joseph

Throughout Scripture we meet other talented individuals with significant God-given abilities who are put to use for God's glory among the nations. Previously we made connections between Daniel and Joseph. Like Daniel, Joseph was forcibly displaced but wound up serving in a foreign court—in his case, Egypt—where his leadership and administrative gifts were put on display.

These opportunities begin when he was a slave in Potiphar's house: "Potiphar put him in charge of his household, and he entrusted to his care everything he owned" (Gen 39:4). After Joseph's falling out with Potiphar, which gets him thrown into prison, he finds favor with the prison warden, who "put Joseph in charge of all those held in the prison, and he was made responsible for all that was done there" (Gen 39:22).

Following his release from prison and finding favor with Pharaoh, Joseph is given significant responsibilities in the Egyptian administration: "So Pharaoh said to Joseph, 'I hereby put you in charge of the whole land of Egypt'" (Gen 41:41). His responsibilities now include managing the national food supply during a time in which Egypt went from experiencing abundant harvests to famine. Through his shrewd management of the food stores, Joseph saves many Egyptians and people from the surrounding nations from starvation (Gen 41:46–57).

Designers and Artisans

Once Moses led the people of Israel out of Egypt, part of becoming God's set-apart people was establishing a sacred place of worship where they could be a witness to the nations. Such a project required skilled designers and artisans to build a space worthy of God's name and glory. In Exodus 31, the Lord spoke to Moses about those set apart for this task:

> *See, I have chosen Bezalel son of Uri, the son of Hur, of the tribe of Judah, and I have filled him with the Spirit of God, with wisdom, with understanding, with knowledge and with all kinds of skills—to make artistic designs for work in gold, silver and bronze, to cut and set stones, to work in wood, and to engage in all kinds of crafts. ... I have given ability to all the skilled workers to make everything I have commanded you: the tent of meeting, the ark of the covenant law with the atonement cover on it, and all the other furnishings of the tent—the table and its articles,*

the pure gold lampstand and all its accessories, the altar of incense, the altar of burnt offering and all its utensils, the basin with its stand—and also the woven garments, both the sacred garments for Aaron the priest and the garments for his sons when they serve as priests, and the anointing oil and fragrant incense for the Holy Place. (Exod 31:2–11) [16]

Moses is clear that these were not merely skilled artisans donating their time and abilities for a building project, but they were filled by the Spirit of God and given wisdom for this consecrated work.[17]

Deborah

After Israel's conquest of the land under Joshua and before God gave Israel kings, the Israelites were led by judges. In the book of Judges, we observe multiple cycles in Israel's story from disobedience to renewed faithfulness. The periods of disobedience were captured by this haunting phrase: "The Israelites did evil in the eyes of the LORD" (Judg 3:7).

One outstanding leader during this time was the prophet Deborah (see Judg 4–5). As part of her work as Israel's judge, "She held court under the Palm of Deborah between Ramah and Bethel in the hill country of Ephraim, and the Israelites went up to her to have their disputes decided" (Judg 4:5).

During Israel's losing military campaigns against the Canaanites, she speaks the word of the Lord to Barak, the Israelite commander, to go up and fight the Canaanites. At Barak's request, Deborah accompanies the armies to the battlefield and exhorts them to fight. By God's power, the Israelites emerge victorious, and as judge, Deborah leads the nation in worship: "So may all your enemies perish, LORD! But may all who love you be like the sun when it rises in its strength" (Judg 5:31). Through Deborah's leadership, God blessed Israel, granting the land peace for forty years (Judg 5:31).

David

Once Israel was established as a commonwealth and developed laws that distinguished them as the people of God, the Lord also set apart men and women with the ability to lead. Before he became the king of Israel, David, "a man after [God's] own heart" (1 Sam 13:14), was also a capable military commander under King Saul. In 1 Samuel we read:

---

16 See further Exod 26:1, 31; 28:1–4; 35:30–35.
17 See further Leithart, *Baptism*, 88.

> *Whatever mission Saul sent him on, David was so successful that Saul gave him a high rank in the army. This pleased all the troops, and Saul's officers as well. ...*
>
> *Saul was afraid of David, because the Lord was with David but had departed from Saul. So he sent David away from him and gave him command over a thousand men, and David led the troops in their campaigns. In everything he did he had great success, because the Lord was with him. ... All Israel and Judah loved David, because he led them in their campaigns. (1 Sam 18:5, 12–16)*

Through God's blessing, David found success and was promoted; however, this success also provoked Saul's jealousy and ultimately led to Saul repeatedly trying to take David's life.

Solomon

Solomon succeeded his father David as king of Israel. The Lord appeared to Solomon in a dream and said, "Ask for whatever you want me to give you" (1 Kgs 3:5). Solomon famously responded with a request for wisdom to lead God's people: "I am only a little child and do not know how to carry out my duties. ... So give your servant a discerning heart to govern your people and to distinguish between right and wrong" (1 Kgs 3:7, 9). God was pleased with Solomon's noble request and promised to not only give him wisdom but also "wealth and honor" (1 Kgs 3:13). The writer of Kings further describes Solomon's wisdom:

> *Solomon's wisdom was greater than the wisdom of all the people of the East, and greater than all the wisdom of Egypt. ... And his fame spread to all the surrounding nations. He spoke three thousand proverbs and his songs numbered a thousand and five. He spoke about plant life, from the cedar of Lebanon to the hyssop that grows out of walls. He also spoke about animals and birds, reptiles and fish. From all nations people came to listen to Solomon's wisdom, sent by all the kings of the world, who had heard of his wisdom. (1 Kgs 4:30–34)*

Solomon displayed his wisdom through administering justice in Israel. The most famous account of this was when Solomon ruled in the dispute between two women over the death of a baby (1 Kgs 3:16–28). Solomon also proved to be a wise and prolific builder. During his reign, he constructed the temple in Jerusalem as well as an opulent palace for himself (1 Kgs 5–6). Finally, he influenced many foreign visitors through his wisdom. His most famous recorded guest (1 Kgs 10:1–13) was the Queen of Sheba (modern Yemen or Ethiopia). As this Gentile leader conversed with Solomon, she would have learned about Israel's God. This meeting was a good example of Old Testament mission in which peoples from around the world came up to Israel to encounter Israel's God.[18]

Nehemiah

A century after Daniel's death, Nehemiah, who served as cupbearer to the Persian King Artaxerxes, demonstrated courageous leadership during the repatriation of Jews and the rebuilding of the wall of Jerusalem. Before the rebuilding project could even begin, Nehemiah courageously communicated the situation in Jerusalem to Artaxerxes: "May the king live forever! Why should my face not look sad when the city where my ancestors are buried lies in ruins, and its gates have been destroyed by fire?" (Neh 2:3). Receiving favor from the king, Nehemiah was allowed leave from his work as cupbearer, granted safe passage to Jerusalem, given materials to rebuild the wall, and effectively appointed governor over Jerusalem (Neh 2:6–9).

Once in Jerusalem, Nehemiah conducted a covert nighttime survey of the wall and developed a plan for its repair. Communicating vision for the work among the returned Jewish exiles, Nehemiah declared: "Come, let us rebuild the wall of Jerusalem" (Neh 2:17). Having recruited these volunteer laborers, Nehemiah led an aggressive fifty-two-day rebuilding project in the face of the active opposition of Sanballat the Horonite, Tobiah the Ammonite official, and Geshem the Arab (Neh 2:19–20; 4:1–23; 6:1–19).

With the wall completed, Nehemiah continued in his role as governor. In this role, he fought for justice for the poor and later carried out other reforms that would restore Jerusalem as a city on a hill and a light to the nations (Neh 5:1–19; 10:1; 13:1–31).

One of the remarkable things about the mission of God in the Old Testament is that it was not primarily accomplished by priests but by professionals—government administrators, military leaders, kings, and other skilled laborers. While each person possessed natural abilities, these abilities were God-given and to be used for God's glory among the nations.

---

18 See further Wright, *Mission of God*, 523.

Natural Abilities for Mission in History

In church and mission history, we meet many self-identifying missionaries who possessed significant natural abilities that contributed to the work of mission. We also meet other committed believers whose skills and strategic positions in society also allowed them to maintain a meaningful witness.

Church of the East Monks and Merchants

The primary church movement that flourished in Arabia and Persia in the third century was the Church of the East—Syrian and Persian Christians who lived between Edessa and Nisibis in the border region between the Roman and Persian Empires.[19] As the Church of the East expanded from Persia to Central Asia and even to China in the seventh and eighth centuries, two groups emerged that participated in mission—merchants and monks. Church of the East merchants conducted business along the Silk Road, actively proclaiming the gospel as they went. Because of their faithful witness, the Syriac word for "merchant" became synonymous, over time, with the word for "missionary."

Church of the East monks established hundreds of monasteries and new churches in the major cities along the Silk Road, making the church the most vital expression of Christianity east of Antioch following the rise of Islam. Though the Silk Road environment could be dangerous and was populated with traders intent on making money, the monks lived very simply: their possessions amounted to coats, sacred books, and walking sticks. Each time they established a new monastery, the monks would invite the local population to take part in the community's manual labor, which led to new relationships and opportunities to share the gospel.

The monks employed a holistic approach to ministry, which included showing hospitality, setting up schools, and offering medical care. Many monasteries functioned as small hospitals and became known to the local communities as healing places. Other monasteries, particularly those established in Western China, contained significant libraries, with books on medicine and philosophy, Bible commentaries, sacred biographies of saints and martyrs, and copies of Scripture.[20]

Matteo Ricci

During the sixteenth century, when China was considered closed to all outsiders, including Christian missionaries, the Italian Jesuit missionary, Matteo Ricci (1552–1610), managed to gain access. Ricci was initially sent

---

19 See further Baum and Winkler, *Church of the East*.
20 See further Smither, *Missionary Monks*, 138–47.

to Macao, an island off the Chinese mainland where the Portuguese set up trade, to study Chinese and wait for the opportunity to enter. In 1583, Ricci received an invitation to live in the provincial capital of Zhaoqing. Later, in 1600, he moved to Peking (Beijing), where he resided until his death ten years later.

Though Ricci was challenged by his superior to prepare for ministry in China, it was Ricci's unique training and professional skills that allowed him access. Having trained in the sciences, Ricci became a qualified astronomer, and the Chinese government paid him an annual stipend to work in the royal observatory. When Ricci first came to China, he brought clocks as gifts for the Chinese leaders, who were very interested in this technology. Not only was he skilled in building clocks, but he could repair and maintain them as well, which made his presence even more valued by the Chinese.

Finally, Ricci was trained in mapmaking. Because China had been isolated from the rest of the world, many Chinese intellectuals were curious to learn more about the greater world and thus valued Ricci's contribution. Known for adopting Chinese dress and customs and ministering to Chinese intellectuals, Ricci gained credibility because of his training in science and cartography. Through Ricci's witness, over two thousand Chinese believed in Christ, including members of the royal family and leading scholars.[21]

William Wilberforce

In 1780, while still a student at Cambridge University, William Wilberforce (1759–1833) was elected to the British parliament. Though initially motivated to enter politics because of personal ambition, after his conversion, in 1786, Wilberforce was driven by his Christian convictions. Wilberforce lived during the height of the global slave trade in the eighteenth and early-nineteenth centuries. It was difficult for many people, including committed Christians, to imagine the economy of the British Empire functioning without slave labor.

Convicted that all people were created in God's image, Wilberforce made it his life's work, in parliament, to put an end to the slave trade. He wrote,

> *So enormous, so dreadful, so irremediable did the [slave] trade's wickedness appear that my own mind was completely made up for abolition. Let the consequences be what they would: I from this time determined that I would never rest until I had effected its abolition.*[22]

---

21 See further Smither, 172–73.
22 "William Wilberforce: Antislavery Politician."

Finally, in 1807, Great Britain voted to end the slave trade. Then, in 1833, just three days before Wilberforce's death, the Slavery Abolition Act was passed that freed slaves throughout most of the British Empire.

Wilberforce also labored for social transformation within the British context. A member of the "Clapham Sect, a group of devout Christians of influence in government and business,"[23] Wilberforce advocated for the poor, orphans, and the uneducated, among others. He also helped found a number of charities and mission organizations, including the Society for Bettering the Cause of the Poor, the Church Missionary Society (an Anglican evangelical mission), and the British and Foreign Bible Society.[24]

Kenneth Cragg

Following in the way of Daniel, who was well educated in the literature and culture of the Babylonians, Kenneth Cragg (1913–2012) became a winsome model for Christian witness among Muslims because of his commitment to study. An Anglican bishop, Cragg served Anglican congregations in Jerusalem, Cairo, Beirut, and Nigeria, as well as in his native Great Britain.

In addition to his Christian theological training, Cragg mastered Arabic and became a world-renowned scholar of the Qur'an. In fact, Muslim scholars often sought out Bishop Cragg for his perspectives on the Qur'an and Islamic theology. Cragg authored over fifty books that compared and contrasted Christian and Muslim thought. He urged Christians to learn what Muslims believe, cultivate a sincere appreciation for Muslim beliefs and traditions, and strive to build honest friendships with Muslims. Building on this basis of friendship and understanding, a Christian could sustain meaningful dialogues with Muslims and even invite them to follow Christ. Cragg later served as the editor of the *Muslim World* journal and taught Arabic and Islamic Studies at Hartford Seminary.[25]

Natural Abilities for Contemporary Mission

Tentmaking and Business as Mission

Over the past few decades, missionaries—particularly those going to serve in closed countries where the gospel cannot be freely proclaimed—have embraced tentmaking.[26] That is, they have acquired professional

---

23 "Wilberforce: Antislavery Politician."
24 See further "Wilberforce: Antislavery Politician."
25 See further Kerr, "Cragg, Albert Kenneth."
26 See further Wilson, *Today's Tentmakers*; also Lai, *Tentmaking*.

skills and credentials to be able to reside and work in such contexts. Many tentmakers have served as English teachers, university professors, nurses, or businesspeople, or have started nonprofit organizations.

A friend of mine worked as an accountant but also sensed a burden to serve the Lord in cross-cultural ministry. After attending seminary and joining a mission organization, he found a job in the accounting department of an international company with an office in a restricted country. Later he worked for a national company, before launching his own accounting firm.

During his professional journey, my friend strived to reconcile a call to serve in mission with his desire to work in accounting. What he discovered was that his professional training allowed him legitimate access into the country, as well as credibility to remain there. At one point, the government began expelling expatriates from the country because of their missionary activity, including many who did not have legitimate employment. Because of the value my friend's company brought to the country, he was allowed to remain. Finally, because the workplace is a relational space, he bonded with others on the job and was able to share the gospel naturally with them. In short, his missionary and professional callings were quite compatible.

In the realm of global business, the tentmaking approach has matured in recent years to a strategy known as business as mission (BAM). The BAM Global Think Tank has used the following working definition.

Business as mission is:

- Profitable and sustainable businesses;
- Intentional about kingdom-of-God purpose and impact on people and nations;
- Focused on holistic transformation and the multiple bottom lines of economic, social, environmental, and spiritual outcomes;
- Concerned about the world's poorest and least-evangelized peoples.[27]

While many in the international business community participate in BAM initiatives, BAM practitioners seem to be, first and foremost, missionaries who desire to bring gospel transformation to societies through business.[28]

---

27 Plummer, "What Is Business as Mission?"
28 See further "BAM Global"; also Lai, *Business for Transformation*.

Strategically Placed Professionals

Daniel's model of mission seems to refer more to believers already placed in their vocation who have a witness for the Lord. For example, I know a Brazilian man who worked for a South American company with an office in the Middle East. Though he moved to the region simply to work, he realized that he had many opportunities to share the gospel with Arab Muslims during his workday. On trips abroad, he began purchasing Bibles to bring to friends. Eventually he and some colleagues started a church that was attended by both international workers and local Muslim friends.

> *Daniel's model of mission seems to refer more to believers already placed in their vocation who have a witness for the Lord.*

Another Latin American believer, a professional sports agent, moved to the Middle East, where he represented international soccer players. Through this very relational industry, he shared his faith regularly and began to see Muslim friends follow Christ. Eventually, he also started a church, with new believers, in his home. Not seeing himself as a missionary, per se, he wrote back to his home church in Latin America, asking them to send a pastor or missionary. What he did not realize was that he was probably the most strategic missionary for the sports community in his context.

Following the legacy of William Wilberforce, many Christians continue to serve in elected and appointed positions in government. When I lived in North Africa and Europe, I knew several ambassadors and diplomatic staff who were committed followers of Christ. A former British ambassador became an advocate for religious freedom for North African Christians from Muslim backgrounds. At one point, the national church, which typically met in homes because of lack of freedom to meet publicly, was encountering pressure from the local police because of its secret gatherings. Learning about this, the ambassador and his legal counsel studied the situation. As a result, they sent a letter to the national church inviting them to meet for worship at the Anglican Church, a property owned by the British government.

Some professionals graciously share their expertise in mission and community-development contexts. A retired professor of environmental engineering at a prestigious American university spends hours each week consulting with community-development specialists around the world about best practices in clean-water projects. A group of Christian doctors in Atlanta give time every week to run a clinic for refugees who lack the resources for medical care.

These strategically trained and placed professionals are the Daniels of twenty-first-century mission. While their skills are greatly needed and highly valued, very few would identify themselves as missionaries.

Summary: Toward Leveraging Natural Abilities in Mission

Daniel and his three friends were healthy, well-educated, and gifted with God-given natural abilities, which allowed them to be a witness for God in Babylon and Persia. Though they were devout Jewish believers, they were not priests or professional religious workers. Daniel's model for mission challenges the modern traditional paradigm of mission participation. While we have often celebrated the place and service of professional ministers and missionaries, the global church must also learn to celebrate the role of those with natural and professional skills who are serving in the marketplace and public square, where they can be a witness for Christ.

The global church must recognize that all work (in education, business, government, church) ought to be worship. We witness unto Christ through the excellent job we do and the godly character we demonstrate. For Adam and Eve in the garden of Eden, their workplace and place of worship were the same. If our work is worship, then it can also be a powerful means to witness for Christ. In the twenty-first century, the witness of a medical doctor, ambassador, or professional soccer coach may be better received than that of a minister.

God's people must also be "salt and light" (Matt 5:13–14) in all spheres of society. In a speech in 1880, the Dutch theologian Abraham Kuyper (1837–1920) declared, "There is not a square inch in the whole domain of our human existence over which Christ, who is Sovereign over all, does not cry, 'Mine!'"

Since God is sovereign and has also given the cultural mandate to "Be fruitful and increase in number; fill the earth and subdue it" (Gen 1:28), God's people ought to glorify him in every domain of society. This includes government, education, the arts, the marketplace, and the family. Kuyper modeled this himself by serving as a Dutch Reformed minister, founding a newspaper and a political party, launching a university, and later serving as the prime minister of the Netherlands.[29] Mission in the way of Daniel invites Christians to pursue their calling and to glorify God in these domains.

We must also recognize that all mission work should be holistic. As we make God's glory known among all nations, we care about the whole person—his or her spiritual, emotional, physical, and economic needs. Missionaries may lead the way in caring for spiritual needs, but other professionals (e.g., counselors, nurses, social entrepreneurs, and government officials) possess unique skills to minister to the whole person also.

When missionaries are going out for the first time, or perhaps returning to their field of service, their church leaders will call them forward, lay hands on them, and pray for God's blessing on their work. This is a wonderful and necessary practice that involves the whole church in global mission, and it ought to continue. Given the mission model of Daniel, we should also lay hands on and pray for doctors, teachers, social workers, engineers, agricultural specialists, and other professionals as they go out into their place of work and ministry.

Questions for Reflection

1. When we consider the model of Daniel, a believer who was not a priest or "religious professional," how does that challenge or shape our notion of what a missionary is?

2. What is the relationship between possessing excellent natural abilities and training and having a witness for Christ in society?

3. How might Christian professionals in the global marketplace, or public square, be encouraged to be "salt and light"?

4. After reading this chapter, what new thoughts do you have about your occupation and place of work? What steps of faith can you take this week?

---

29 See further Ashford, *Every Square Inch*; also Mouw, *Abraham Kuyper*; and Wagenman, *Engaging the World*.

CHAPTER 3

Favored: God-Given Favor before Authorities

Sometimes it's easy to forget that Daniel was a displaced person whose homeland had been attacked. He received the finest education one could find in Babylon, and he clearly possessed natural, God-given abilities to succeed in his adopted country. In addition to his gifts and abilities, Daniel found repeated favor with the authorities in Babylon, and later in Persia, which allowed him to flourish and also have a witness for Israel's God.

Ashpenaz

Shortly after the siege of Jerusalem, Daniel found favor with the Babylonian court official Ashpenaz, who was tasked by Nebuchadnezzar with gathering members of the royal family and nobility for service in Babylon. As we've read, Daniel was troubled by the diet that was planned for the exiles, and he courageously approached his captor for a dietary exemption:

> But Daniel resolved not to defile himself with the royal food and wine, and he asked the chief official for permission not to defile himself this way. Now God had caused the official to show favor and compassion to Daniel, but the official

> told Daniel, "I am afraid of my lord the king, who has assigned your food and drink. Why should he see you looking worse than the other young men your age? The king would then have my head because of you." (Dan 1:8–10)

The Hebrew word *ḥesed*, translated "favor" in this Scripture passage, can also mean "mercy," "kindness," "faithfulness," or "loyalty." As people placed their trust in Israel's God, the Lord showed them his mercy and lovingkindness. In this context, one human being—in this case, a person in authority—is showing mercy and kindness to another person.

Consistent with the theme of divine sovereignty throughout the book of Daniel, God works sovereignly in the heart of the Babylonian official who shows Daniel favor. Goldingay asserts, "For a Gentile court official to be so accommodating was a sufficiently remarkable and unusual experience to require explanation."[1] Longman adds, "The true God is the One who orchestrates events for the good of his people."[2]

Though sympathetic, Ashpenaz makes no promises to Daniel. Understanding the court official's predicament before King Nebuchadnezzar, Daniel craftily approaches the guard assigned to him and his companions, and he makes a deal:

> Daniel then said to the guard whom the chief official had appointed over Daniel, Hananiah, Mishael and Azariah, "Please test your servants for ten days: Give us nothing but vegetables to eat and water to drink. Then compare our appearance with that of the young men who eat the royal food, and treat your servants in accordance with what you see." So he agreed to this and tested them for ten days.
>
> At the end of the ten days they looked healthier and better nourished than any of the young men who ate the royal food. So the guard took away their choice food and the wine they were to drink and gave them vegetables instead. (Dan 1:11–16)

Not only does God give Daniel favor both with Ashpenaz and the guard to even consider their request, but God also blesses them physically so they can continue this habit of not eating food that would defile them and keep them from being God's set-apart ones in Babylon. While Shadrach, Meshach, and Abednego will show courage in the fiery furnace saga,

---

1 Goldingay, *Daniel*, 26.

2 Longman, *Daniel*, 54.

Daniel seems to take the lead in following this austere path that requires God's favor and the Babylonian officials' favor.

Nebuchadnezzar

Daniel also finds favor with King Nebuchadnezzar when he is called upon to interpret his first dream in the narrative chapters. Nebuchadnezzar has a troubling dream and gives his wise men an impossible task—not just to interpret it but to recount it in the first place (Dan 2:1–11). When the Babylonian sages are not up to the task, the king becomes livid and orders "the execution of all the wise men of Babylon" (Dan 2:12), which includes Daniel.

Daniel finds favor initially with Arioch, the "commander of the king's guard" (Dan 2:14), who was responsible for arresting and executing the sages. In the text we read that "Daniel spoke to him with wisdom and tact. He asked the king's officer, 'Why did the king issue such a harsh decree?' Arioch then explained the matter to Daniel" (Dan 2:14b–15). The fact that Daniel could even have a conversation with Arioch implies some degree of favor. Perhaps they had a personal relationship or God gave Arioch a willingness to listen to Daniel.

Since Arioch is willing to listen, Daniel speaks to him with "wisdom and tact," which earns him an audience with King Nebuchadnezzar: "Daniel went in to the king and asked for time, so that he might interpret the dream for him" (Dan 2:16).[3] Given the king's angry disposition, Daniel's brief audience with the king demonstrates even more favor. His request for time to interpret the dream was also significant, since the other Babylonian sages were not granted that.[4]

Through God's power, Daniel successfully interprets Nebuchadnezzar's dream and is favored even more by the king.

> *Then King Nebuchadnezzar fell prostrate before Daniel and paid him honor and ordered that an offering and incense be presented to him. ...*
>
> *Then the king placed Daniel in a high position and lavished many gifts on him. He made him ruler over the entire province of Babylon and placed him in charge of all its wise men. Moreover, at Daniel's request the king appointed Shadrach, Meshach and Abednego administrators over the province of Babylon, while Daniel himself remained at the royal court. (Dan 2:46–49)*

---

3 See further Longman, *Daniel*, 78; also Goldingay, *Daniel*, 55.
4 See further Goldingay, *Daniel*, 55; also Fernando, *Spiritual Living*, 41.

Though it may appear that the king is worshiping Daniel in this passage, the better explanation is that the king is paying Daniel homage and "honoring a benefactor" through bowing down and offering gifts.[5] The king continues to show Daniel favor by promoting him to greater leadership in Babylon and over the wise men. Through Daniel's recommendation, Nebuchadnezzar shows favor to Shadrach, Meshach, and Abednego in their assignments as administrators.[6]

Following their miraculous survival of the furnace, Shadrach, Meshach, and Abednego receive increased favor from Nebuchadnezzar as well. Praising their God and their faith, the king decrees that "the people of any nation or language who say anything against the God of Shadrach, Meshach and Abednego be cut into pieces and their houses be turned into piles of rubble, for no other god can save in this way" (Dan 3:29). The king shows the men favor by protecting them but also by threatening to harm those who oppose them and their God. He also promotes them to greater roles within the empire.

Darius

Daniel also experienced favor with Darius the Mede before and after the famous lions' den incident. Tricked by Daniel's political enemies into issuing a decree forbidding prayer to anyone but Darius for thirty days, Darius could not change the law even though it implicated Daniel. The king tells Daniel: "May your God, whom you serve continually, rescue you!" (Dan 6:16). While Darius's communication is ambiguous—hopeful and supportive though unwilling to overturn the law—the fact that he cares at all for Daniel indicates some level of favor.[7]

After Daniel survives the night in the lions' den, Darius extends favor by releasing him and punishing Daniel's accusers: "At the king's command, the men who had falsely accused Daniel were brought in and thrown into the lions' den, along with their wives and children. And before they reached the floor of the den, the lions overpowered them and crushed all their bones" (Dan 6:24).

Similar to the account of the fiery furnace, those who had falsely accused the Judean exile are punished, while Daniel, like his companions

---

5 Goldingay, *Daniel*, 52; see also Longman, *Daniel*, 84.

6 See further Goldingay, *Daniel*, 52; also Longman, *Daniel*, 83.

7 See further Goldingay, 132, 135; also Longman, 162.

before him, is shown favor.[8] The lions' den narrative concludes with Daniel being shown more favor: "So Daniel prospered during the reign of Darius and the reign of Cyrus the Persian" (Dan 6:28).

Just because Daniel and the other Hebrews were exiles did not mean that they could not flourish.[9] They flourished because they possessed God-given natural abilities and were educated, but also because they found favor with the ruling authorities in Babylon and later in Persia. Because of this favor, they also had many opportunities to be a witness for the God of Israel in a foreign land.

God-Given Favor for Mission in Scripture

Joseph

Throughout the broader story of Scripture, God's mission and ways continue because God gives his people favor among unbelieving leaders and authorities.[10] While Joseph demonstrated remarkable leadership abilities, his success in Egypt was ultimately based on the favor God gave him among the Egyptians.

The text richly conveys that Joseph experienced favor from the outset of his time in Egypt in the household of Potiphar, the man who bought him from the Ishmaelites:

> *The LORD was with Joseph so that he prospered, and he lived in the house of his Egyptian master. When his master saw that the LORD was with him and that the LORD gave him success in everything he did, Joseph found favor in his eyes and became his attendant. Potiphar put him in charge of his household, and he entrusted to his care everything he owned. (Gen 39:2–4)*

"Favor" (Hebrew *ḥen*) in this passage can also be translated as "grace" or "kindness." Because of this divine favor, Joseph not only experienced success and promotion, but his work brought blessing to Potiphar's house and work.

Though Joseph's place in Potiphar's house was short-lived because of false accusations of sexual impropriety brought by Potiphar's wife, he continued to find favor in prison: "But while Joseph was there in the prison, the LORD was with him; he showed him kindness and granted him

---

8   See further Goldingay, *Daniel*, 126, 134–35.
9   See further Fernando, *Spiritual Living*, 19.
10 See further Goldingay, *Daniel*, 26.

favor in the eyes of the prison warden" (Gen 39:20–21). This favor (ḥesed) translated into further opportunities for Joseph to show his abilities, as the warden placed him in charge of the prison operations.

Word of Joseph's dream-interpreting skills eventually reached Pharaoh, who was in need of such services. Joseph's God-given wisdom and discernment gave him favor with Pharaoh, who placed Joseph in charge of his palace and the entire land of Egypt (Gen 41:1–41).

Nehemiah

Like Joseph, Nehemiah demonstrated the ability to lead; however, his work was made possible because of favor from the Persian King Artaxerxes. Before going before the king, Nehemiah prayed for "favor in the presence of this man" (Neh 1:11). Here "favor" (raḥamim) signifies "mercy" or "compassion."

When the king notices his cupbearer's depressed countenance and inquires about it (that alone was a form of favor), Nehemiah has the courage to speak up: "Why should my face not look sad when the city where my ancestors are buried lies in ruins, and its gates have been destroyed by fire?" (Neh 2:3). Artaxerxes and his queen extend further favor by asking Nehemiah "What is it you want?" (Neh 2:4). And then the king asks Nehemiah how much time he needs for the Jerusalem rebuilding project. The king grants Nehemiah time away from his duties at court, letters of safe passage to Jerusalem, and building material to reconstruct the wall (Neh 2:4–9).

While Nehemiah's project was ultimately successful, thus aiding the Israelites to repatriate and be once more the people of God and a light to the nations, the work began with God-given favor from a nonbelieving Persian king.

Esther

Esther's story is yet another account of God glorifying his name among the Gentiles through the witness of diaspora Jews. Esther was a Judean exile raised by her cousin Mordecai in the Persian city of Susa. When Queen Vashti is deposed by King Xerxes, Esther is placed in a harem of young women, one of whom Xerxes would select to be the next queen. There she found favor with Hegai, "who had charge of the harem" (Esth 2:8–9). Because of Mordecai's counsel, Esther keeps her Jewish identity a secret (Esth 2:5–10).

Esther experiences favor from Xerxes by being selected as his queen:

> *Now the king was attracted to Esther more than to any of the other women, and she won his favor and approval more than any of the other virgins. So he set a royal crown on her head and made her queen instead of Vashti. (Esth 2:17)*

Like Daniel and his three fellow exiles, Esther undergoes a period of training and preparation before being set apart for the king.[11] Shortly after her coronation, she blesses her husband and the royal court by conveying news of a conspiracy to assassinate the king, a plot that was uncovered by Mordecai (Esth 2:21–23).

Esther receives even greater favor from King Xerxes when she risks her life to intervene and save her fellow Jews from genocide. Haman, an Amalekite—a people who had longstanding scores to settle with the Jews—had been elevated to one of the highest places of leadership in the kingdom. From this position, he convinces the king to issue an edict to exterminate the Jews in Persia (Esth 3).

At this point, Esther enters the king's presence uninvited, which could have cost her life. Xerxes responds by extending his gold scepter, a sign of favor. He asks, "What is it, Queen Esther? What is your request? Even up to half the kingdom, it will be given you" (Esth 5:3). As the saga continues, Esther denounces Haman's wicked plan to destroy the Jews, while also revealing her own Jewish identity. She pleads with the king,

> *If I have found favor with you, Your Majesty, and if it pleases you, grant me my life—this is my petition. And spare my people—this is my request. For I and my people have been sold to be destroyed, killed and annihilated. (Esth 7:3–4)*

Xerxes responds by having Haman executed. After Haman's death, Esther once again enters Xerxes' presence; and he extends his scepter a second time. This time, she appeals to the king to have the edict to exterminate the Jews overturned. Because of his loyalty to the king, Mordecai is favored, elevated, and given the king's seal to rewrite the edict (Esth 8). As the narrative closes, both Esther and Mordecai find favor in Persia (Esth 9:29–10:3).

Through the God-given favor extended to Esther by Xerxes, the Jewish people are delivered from extermination, an event remembered

---

11 See further Fewell, *Circle of Sovereignty*, 16.

by the Feast of Purim. By bringing to light a plot to kill the king, Esther and Mordecai preserve Xerxes' life and also bless the Persian Empire. Because of Esther and Mordecai's godly lives and actions, the Persians witness the reality and power of Israel's God.

People of Peace

Whenever Jesus sent out his disciples for mission during his earthly ministry, their ministry would depend on people of peace. In Luke's Gospel, Jesus instructs: "When you enter a house, first say, 'Peace to this house.' If someone who promotes peace is there, your peace will rest on them; if not, it will return to you" (Luke 10:5–6). In one sense, people of peace offered hospitality and provided for the physical needs of the itinerant apostles. In another sense, they were people with influence who facilitated the ministry and enabled the apostles to reach a broader audience.

> *Whether or not Gamaliel is sympathetic to the apostles' message, he convinces the Sanhedrin to restrain from killing them. As a result, the apostles become bolder and continue preaching the gospel.*

Such people of peace may or may not have been God-fearers, but they were led by God to extend favor. A number of people of peace can be observed aiding the New Testament church on mission. One such man was Gamaliel, a devout Jew and member of the Sanhedrin. In Acts 5, Luke records Peter and the apostles being imprisoned, escaping from prison, and being beaten for preaching Christ in Jerusalem. When commanded by the Sanhedrin to stop preaching Christ, they declare, "We must obey God rather than human beings!" (Acts 5:29).

When the members of the Sanhedrin discuss putting the apostles to death, Gamaliel speaks up and urges prudence. He reminds them of other rebel religious leaders who had come and gone and concludes: "Leave these men alone! Let them go! For if their purpose or activity is of human origin, it will fail. But if it is from God, you will not be able to stop these men; you will only find yourselves fighting against God" (Acts 5:38–39). Whether or not Gamaliel is sympathetic to the apostles' message, he convinces the Sanhedrin to restrain from killing them. As a result, the apostles become bolder and continue preaching the gospel.

During his journey to Rome for trial, the Apostle Paul and his missionary band encountered people of peace on the island of Malta after they were shipwrecked. Luke writes, "The islanders showed us unusual kindness. They built a fire and welcomed us all because it was raining and cold" (Acts 28:2). Paul's brief stay in Malta was marked by miracles and healing, but it was also facilitated by the hospitality of the Maltese. Luke continues:

> *There was an estate nearby that belonged to Publius, the chief official of the island. He welcomed us to his home and showed us generous hospitality for three days. His father was sick in bed, suffering from fever and dysentery. Paul went in to see him and, after prayer, placed his hands on him and healed him. When this had happened, the rest of the sick on the island came and were cured. They honored us in many ways; and when we were ready to sail, they furnished us with the supplies we needed. (Acts 28:7–10)*

The Maltese welcome not only enabled Paul's ministry among the islanders, but also allowed Paul to have a witness among the Roman guards who were escorting him to trial in Rome.

God-Given Favor in Mission History

As we scan the pages of mission history, we discover that the mission of God was also facilitated by many other people of peace. In some cases, these were nonbelieving monarchs who welcomed missionaries to make the gospel known among their subjects.

Missionary Monks

One of the strategies of missionary monks, the most prominent group of missionaries in church history between around AD 400 and 1600, was first to approach tribal leaders and kings and seek their favor before proclaiming Christ in their domains. Patrick of Ireland initiated ministry in a new area by first approaching tribal or political leaders. Robert Wilken asserts, "In Ireland the basic social unit was a tribe or clan under a king without any fixed territory. ... By making alliances with the local dynasties Patrick was able to advance the Christian mission."[12]

As Patrick continued to mix with such leaders and build relationships, some of them embraced the gospel. Patrick also recruited the sons of some kings to travel with him as guides and mediators on potentially

---
12 Wilken, *First Thousand Years*, 271.

treacherous journeys. Patrick's actions reveal that he was serving in contexts of violence, and he understood how to navigate the social and power structures of fifth-century Ireland in order to preach the gospel.[13]

The missionary work of the Irish monk Columba (520–97) began around 565, when he made contact with the Pictish King Brute. Venerable Bede wrote that Columba

> *came to Britain to preach the word of God to the kingdoms of the northern Picts. ... Columba came to Britain when Bridius [Brute] ... a most powerful king, had been ruling over them for over eight years. Columba turned them to the faith of Christ by his words and example and so received the island of Iona from them in order to establish a monastery there.*[14]

Before believing the gospel himself, King Brute granted Columba the right to preach the gospel among the Pictish people and helped make that possible by giving the abbot the island of Iona as a physical base for monastic living and for mission among the Picts. Since Columba descended from royalty in Ireland, he seemed more comfortable than other monks interacting with kings and those in authority in the British Isles.[15] While doing a thorough job of evangelizing the Picts during Columba's lifetime, the monastic community at Iona continued to evangelize the British Isles and Europe for the next three centuries.

The mission to evangelize the English in 596, initiated by Bishop Gregory of Rome and led by the monk Augustine of Canterbury, was largely based on the favor of English monarchs. When Augustine arrived in England, he first approached King Ethelbert of Kent. Although Ethelbert did not initially embrace the gospel for himself, he did give the monks space to build a church and monastery for their own worship and also as a base for their ministry. He also granted them freedom to preach among his people.

Gregory's initiative to send a team of missionary monks to England probably came at the invitation of Queen Bertha, a Christian from Gaul, who would have already influenced her nonbelieving husband to consider the gospel. According to Gregory, in the first year of the mission more than ten thousand English believed the gospel and were baptized; and as a result, Canterbury became the heart of the church in England.[16]

---

13 Robert, *Christian Mission*, 153; also Smither, *Missionary Monks*, 51–63.

14 Bede, *Ecclesiastical History*, 115.

15 See further McNeill, *Celtic Churches*, 90; also Smither, *Missionary Monks*, 64–70.

16 See further Bede, *Ecclesiastical History* 1.25–26; also Smither, *Missionary Monks*, 82–92.

Europe wasn't the only place where we witness this dynamic. Though the Mongol Empire, led by Genghis Khan and his sons, violently dominated Central and East Asia for most of the thirteenth and fourteenth centuries, the khans were tolerant of Christianity. Beginning in the middle of the thirteenth century, the khans invited Christian teachers—mostly Dominican and Franciscan friars—to preach the gospel among the Mongols and also to minister to Church of the East Christians living in the Mongol Empire.

In 1289, Pope Nicolas IV sent the Franciscan John of Montecorvino all the way to China to reach out to the khan. Though the Mongol leader converted to Buddhism, he still allowed Montecorvino much freedom to preach the gospel among his people. The friar reportedly baptized some six thousand Mongols and started a church, making his mission the most fruitful work in the thirteenth century among this Asian people.[17]

Timothy of Baghdad

Finally, Timothy of Baghdad (727–823), the Church of the East bishop, experienced favor with the Muslim Caliph Mahdi to proclaim Christ freely and to send out Christian missionaries. Timothy began leading the church in Baghdad in 762, a little more than a decade after the Abbasid Dynasty established its caliphate (global ruling center for Islam) in the city. Trained in theology and philosophy, the bishop was well equipped to respond to the objections Muslim leaders in Baghdad had with the gospel.

In 781, Caliph Mahdi offered the bishop protection and a safe space for a two-day open dialogue about their respective faiths. Timothy freely responded to Muslim concerns about the gospel, including the matter of God having a son, of Christians worshiping three gods, and of whether or not Muhammad was mentioned in the Bible. Without attacking Islam or the Prophet Muhammad, Timothy boldly presented historic Christian teaching in the peaceful yet frank dialogue.[18]

In addition to Timothy's local mission in Baghdad, he also found favor with the caliph to send missionaries to the formerly Christian lands in Central and East Asia. Timothy used the Church of the East monasteries in Persia as training centers where monks studied theology, philosophy, medicine, and linguistics in order to preach, care for physical needs, and translate Scripture. Timothy also set apart bishops for new churches in Central Asia, Tibet, and China.[19]

---

17 See further Smither, *Missionary Monks*, 163–64.
18 See further Smither and Castor, "Timothy I of Baghdad," 197–209.
19 See further Smither, *Missionary Monks*, 143–45.

God-Given Favor in Contemporary Mission

Reflections on mission in resistant and difficult-to-reach parts of the world also reveal instances of God-given favor. Not unlike Daniel in Babylon and Persia, God's people on mission benefit from the favor of nonbelieving people of peace—some of whom serve as government officials. In this section, we consider several examples from ministry in the Muslim world.

Andrew van der Bijl (b. 1928), better known as Brother Andrew, founded the ministry Open Doors, which focused on smuggling Bibles into the communist-bloc countries of the Soviet Union and Eastern Europe during the height of the Cold War. Brother Andrew often experienced favor in his missionary work when border guards uncharacteristically allowed him to enter the country without searching his vehicle or bags. Many of these stories are related in Brother Andrew's autobiography, *God's Smuggler*, originally published in 1964.[20]

After the fall of the Soviet Union and the dissolution of communist rule in Eastern Europe, Brother Andrew and Open Doors began to focus on bringing the gospel to the Muslim world. While Andrew had prayed for God to close the eyes of border guards in the communist bloc, he seemed to take a more open approach with Muslim leaders. For example, when visiting Palestine, he would spend time with the chair of the Palestinian Liberation Organization, Yassar Arafat (1929–2004). Openly sharing Christ with the Palestinian leader, he even gave Arafat a copy of *God's Smuggler*. Andrew reported that on follow-up visits, Arafat requested additional copies of the book to give to his friends.

While visiting the founder of Hezbollah in Lebanon, Joseph Cumming also experienced favor that resulted in many Lebanese Muslims hearing the gospel. Cumming was expecting a five-minute meeting with the Shi'a cleric and prayed about what to say in that brief encounter. He emphasized Jesus laying down his life, shedding his blood, and not retaliating against his enemies—the basis for forgiveness and reconciliation between warring peoples. The cleric wanted to hear more, and the conversation went on for another two hours, during which they discussed the Bible, the Trinity, and the suffering of innocent people in the Arab world. On the matter of suffering, Cumming told the cleric:

> *I look at the suffering of all innocent victims of violence and oppression and injustice, regardless of whether they are Israeli, or Palestinian, or Lebanese, or American, through the lens of the suffering and death of Jesus Christ. If it were not for the suffering*

---

20 Brother Andrew, *God's Smuggler*.

> *and death of Jesus Christ, I might wonder at times whether God had abandoned the human race, whether God cared. But in the sufferings of Jesus Christ, I see the sign of God's solidarity with all innocent victims of violence and suffering and oppression.*[21]

After their meeting, Hezbollah put together a video for their television channel filled with images of Christ from the film *The Passion of the Christ*, as well as images of suffering Arabs. Along with the video, Hezbollah issued a press release that said, "The suffering of Jesus Christ is a universal theme. It is something in which everyone, including Muslims, believes."[22]

Though Saddam Hussein (1937–2006) is remembered for his ruthless leadership in Iraq, including going to war with Iran and invading Kuwait, at times he showed favor to the minority Christian communities in his country, which promoted the gospel. During the 1990s, one ministry based in Iraq applied for permission to print two hundred thousand Bibles for distribution throughout the country. Permission was granted, and the Bible campaign went forward.

In a more personal account, a member of Saddam's family was very ill and in the hospital. A Christian visited the relative in the hospital, prayed for them, and the person experienced healing. Over the next week, large trucks sent from the president's palace were dispatched to the Christian churches around Baghdad, delivering supplies and materials to help those congregations in their ministries.

Although religious freedom is generally restricted in the Muslim world—particularly to those who leave Islam for another faith, such as Christianity—at times favor has been extended for religious freedom. A discipleship-training event took place in Egypt in the 1980s that included believers from both Christian and Muslim backgrounds. Police informants had infiltrated the training, and soon many of the participants were put in jail. Word of this reached an American Christian leader attending a reception with then-Vice-President George H. W. Bush, who was on his way to Egypt for a state visit. The church leader found favor with Vice President Bush, who brought the matter to Egyptian President Hosni Mubarak. Almost immediately, President Mubarak ordered all of the Egyptian prisoners to be freed.

Such advocacy for religious freedom continues to go on around the world, though it is usually done quietly. While Christians continue to suffer and be imprisoned for their faith, we do observe encouraging signs at

---

21 Cumming, "Toward Respectful Witness," 317.
22 Cumming, 318.

times toward religious freedom, and this is often the fruit of favor given by political authorities.

Finally, a number of Christians have run successful businesses and non-governmental organizations (NGOs) in the Muslim world, finding favor for their work and their Christian witness. One individual started an educational NGO in an Arab country. Working on projects aimed to improve education in the country, including starting an international school, he also built relationships with local officials and even members of parliament, who then developed an interest in these projects.

While other international Christian workers in the country generally steered clear of anyone in authority, this man realized that political leaders also need Christ. Though most of his daily ministry occurred amid peronsal relationships, on one occasion he was able to present the king with a copy of St. Augustine's *Confessions* on the king's birthday—a very public event. After the events of September 11, 2001, he was invited to bring a message of peace from the Christian community in this Muslim nation, which was also televised.

Summary: Finding Favor in Mission Today

Mission in the way of Daniel was dependent on favor from those in authority. Of course, it was the Lord who moved in the hearts of these leaders to offer Daniel favor so that God's glory and salvation would be made known to the dispersed Israelites, the Babylonians, the Persians, and the surrounding nations. Such favor was also behind the work of Joseph, Nehemiah, Esther, the apostles, and many others throughout mission history.

What does finding favor in mission look like today? What would pioneer mission work in the least-reached parts of the world look like if we followed the models of Patrick and Columba and first approached the ruling authorities for permission and favor before beginning the work of evangelism and church planting? Patrick's world was no less secure than our present world. He also honored the leaders of Ireland by first meeting with them before beginning his work. As we have seen, he was blessed with their favor. Though I don't advocate that twenty-first-century missionaries act recklessly or put anyone in danger, the principle of favor ought to challenge those who seem to prioritize security above all else in the work of mission.

Seeking the favor of those in authority also reminds us that political leaders (kings, presidents, prime ministers, members of parliament, senators, congressmen, governors, mayors, and state and local officials) all need the Lord. Though there are some excellent ministries to diplomats and political leaders, twenty-first-century mission practitioners must think more about how to make disciples of those in leadership.

Trusting God for favor before political leaders also reflects a vulnerability in mission that challenges narratives of power in global mission. Though Western missionaries often come from politically powerful and wealthy nations, they must not rely on any sense of worldly power as they serve in Africa, Asia, or Latin America. They should seek to bless the city and nation where they are guest workers and trust the Lord for favor with local authorities. Since the majority of cross-cultural missionaries in the world today come from the Global South (Africa, Asia, Latin America), this is less of a temptation for them. Brazilian, Korean, and Mongolian cross-cultural workers will need the favor and blessing of the leaders in their host context.

Finally, just as Jesus instructed his disciples to seek people of peace during their itinerant preaching tours, God's people on mission today should also pray and trust God for people of peace. These are people who welcome missionaries, open doors for the gospel to be proclaimed, invite their friends to hear the gospel, open their home for Bible studies and worship gatherings, and sometimes become leaders of newly planted churches and ministries. Many missionaries today in pioneer mission contexts are actively praying for and seeking people of peace, which is a way of trusting God for favor in mission.[23]

Questions for Reflection

1. How does the idea of God-given favor challenge or shape how you approach mission and ministry?
2. What is the difference between favor, compromise, and bribery?
3. How comfortable are you interacting with those with power and influence in society (i.e., politics, business, cultural influencers) and trusting God for favor to have a witness among them?
4. How has God given you favor in your place of work or your community?
5. How might that favor result in opportunities to be a witness for Christ?

---

23 See further Watson and Watson, *Contagious Disciple Making*, 123–40; also "Persons of Peace."

CHAPTER 4

Empowered: Experiencing and Demonstrating the Power of God in Mission

People crave power and desire control over their lives. This is evident in the actions of political leaders (the democratically elected as well as dictators), military commanders, and corporate executives. It's also true for parents wanting their kids to do their homework, stay out of trouble at school, or go to bed on time. Power and control are also desired by the powerless in this world: a poor domestic worker desiring better hours or pay; a Muslim woman who is the second or third wife in a family, yearning for attention and security; or a refugee family longing to leave a refugee camp in the Middle East for a better life in Europe or the United States.

Religious practices across global religions also reflect a desire for power. People pray for rain, jobs, healthy children, and their political candidates. Many mix those petitions with sacrifices and other rituals—sometimes known as folk or popular religion—to appease their god. They hope and expect their gods to be powerful and to come through for them.

In Daniel's experience as a displaced Israelite in Babylon and Persia, his God demonstrates power over and over. God's power—his mighty supernatural and miraculous acts—stands out as one of the strongest themes in Daniel's missionary experience.

Nebuchadnezzar's First Dream

In Daniel 2, the king's first dream becomes a venue for God to display his power through Daniel. The king had put his sages in an impossible situation, demanding that they interpret the dream without the opportunity even to hear it first. While some have suggested that Nebuchadnezzar had forgotten his dream, it's more likely that the king wanted to ensure his wise men were not making up explanations. In their frustrating back-and-forth with the king, the sages protest, "No one can reveal it to the king except the gods" (Dan 2:11). No human being could fulfill such a request.[1] As we've seen, in response to the king's decision to kill all of his wise men (including Daniel), Daniel gains favor with the king and is given some time to explain the dream.

Realizing this task was beyond his capabilities, Daniel returns home, explains the situation to Shadrach, Meshach, and Abednego, and pleads with them to pray to their God for mercy and wisdom (Dan 2:17–18). In the night, the Lord reveals the meaning of the dream to Daniel (Dan 2:19). While still at home, Daniel exalts the Lord, recognizing God's hand in this mighty act:

> Praise be to the name of God for ever and ever;
> > wisdom and power are his.
> He changes times and seasons;
> > he deposes kings and raises up others.
> He gives wisdom to the wise
> > and knowledge to the discerning.

---

[1] See further Longman, *Daniel*, 77–78; Fewell, *Circle of Sovereignty*, 25; and Goldingay, *Daniel*, 42.

> *He reveals deep and hidden things;*
> > *he knows what lies in darkness,*
> > *and light dwells with him.*
> *I thank and praise you, God of my ancestors:*
> > *You have given me wisdom and power,*
> *you have made known to me what we asked of you,*
> > *you have made known to us the dream of the king.*
> > (Dan 2:20–23)

Daniel praises God for his wisdom, sovereignty over kings and leaders, and for being the revealer of secrets.[2]

Back in the king's presence, Daniel interprets a dream that is very much about power. Nebuchadnezzar's vision of the statue of gold, silver, iron, and clay represents a succession of kingdoms beginning with Nebuchadnezzar's empire and encompassing future ones—probably the Medo-Persians, Greeks, and Romans. While Nebuchadnezzar is confronted with the temporal nature of his rule, Daniel adds that "the God of heaven will set up a kingdom that will never be destroyed. ... It will crush all those kingdoms and bring them to an end. ... This is the meaning of the vision of the rock ..." (Dan 2:44–45).

In the broader witness of Scripture, we understand this rock to be the Lord Jesus Christ, "the rock who establishes God's kingdom by crushing godless nations."[3] Daniel communicates to Nebuchadnezzar that the Most High God is powerful and sovereign over these kingdoms and the kingdoms of the earth. The Babylonian king rules now because God "sets up kings and deposes them."[4]

Nebuchadnezzar's Second Dream

In Daniel 4, Daniel interprets another of the king's dreams, which also has to do with power. Unlike the first dream, Nebuchadnezzar freely recounts the dream to Daniel, perhaps because he has come to trust Daniel. The king also seeks Daniel out for this task because Daniel possesses the "spirit of the holy gods" (Dan 4:9). Though Nebuchadnezzar was not necessarily a believer in Israel's God, the king recognized in Daniel

---

[2] See further Longman, *Daniel*, 73; Fewell, *Circle of Sovereignty*, 28–29; and Goldingay, *Daniel*, 56.

[3] Longman, *Daniel*, 92. See further Ps 118:22; Matt 21:42; Mark 12:10–11; Luke 20:17; Isa 8:14; 28:16; Rom 9:33; 1 Pet 2:6–8.

[4] Longman, *Daniel*, 79; see also Goldingay, *Daniel*, 62.

"the activity of God in his dynamic power, giving life and freedom to his people and to the world" and that Daniel could "behave in remarkable ways and perform extraordinary deeds."[5]

Nebuchadnezzar tells Daniel his dream of a great tree that was cut down and of a man living among animals. Daniel is greatly troubled because this dream is directly related to the king. Nebuchadnezzar had already conquered Jerusalem, Daniel's home city, and now the Judean exile was about to tell the king about the end of his reign.[6] The tree represents the king's power, authority, and rule. Though exalted with a great dominion, the king would be cut down and humbled by the Most High God. Nebuchadnezzar would also go insane, acting like a wild animal.

In the following year the king's dream becomes a reality, as Nebuchadnezzar takes stock of his kingdom and declares: "Is not this the great Babylon I have built as the royal residence, by my mighty power and for the glory of my majesty?" (Dan 4:30).[7] Nebuchadnezzar loses his sanity and is temporarily removed from power until humbling himself before Almighty God.

In Nebuchadnezzar's account of this dream, he introduces and concludes the narrative with words of praise for Daniel's God. Addressing "the nations and peoples of every language, who live in all the earth," the diverse cultural groups in his Babylonian realm, the king writes:

> It is my pleasure to tell you about the miraculous signs and wonders that the Most High God has performed for me.
>
> > How great are his signs,
> > > how mighty his wonders!
> > His kingdom is an eternal kingdom;
> > > his dominion endures from generation to generation.
> > > (Dan 4:2–3)[8]

Having had one dream already interpreted and having seen the deliverance of Shadrach, Meshach, and Abednego from the fiery furnace, Nebuchadnezzar had been greatly impacted by the mighty acts of Daniel's God. Interestingly, he uses the language of "signs and wonders" to

---

5 Goldingay, *Daniel*, 87; see also Longman, *Daniel*, 116; and Fewell, *Circle of Sovereignty*, 65.
6 See further Longman, *Daniel*, 120.
7 See further Fewell, *Circle of Sovereignty*, 71–72.
8 See further Longman, *Daniel*, 118.

describe God's actions. In other parts of Scripture this language refers to God's work delivering Israel from slavery through the Exodus, as well as the actions of the prophets.[9] Once his sanity is restored, Nebuchadnezzar concludes with his own doxology to Daniel's God:

> *At the end of that time, I, Nebuchadnezzar, raised my eyes toward heaven, and my sanity was restored. Then I praised the Most High; I honored and glorified him who lives forever.*
>
> *His dominion is an eternal dominion;*
> > *his kingdom endures from generation to generation. ...*
>
> *All the peoples of the earth*
> > *are regarded as nothing.*
>
> *He does as he pleases*
> > *with the powers of heaven*
> > *and the people of the earth. (Dan 4:34–35)*

In these words, the Babylonian king acknowledges the power of the God of Daniel—the one true God who humbles proud leaders like himself.[10]

Belshazzar and the Handwriting on the Wall

In another act of God's power through Daniel, the prophet is called upon to interpret a message written on the wall of King Belshazzar's banquet hall (Dan 5). King Belshazzar throws a banquet and uses the gold cups taken from the Jerusalem temple. Instead of worshiping the one true God, he offers praise to the gods of gold, silver, bronze, iron, wood, and stone. In some ways a parallel to Nebuchadnezzar's act of building a great image for his subjects to worship, Belshazzar attempts to assert his power over the people of Judah and their God.[11] Longman notes that this is an act of idolatry and blasphemy.[12]

As a result, Belshazzar sees a literal hand writing a message on the wall (Dan 5:5), which he cannot understand—"a supernatural occurrence ... this hand is surely the hand of God."[13] Once more, the Babylonian

---

9 See further Fewell, *Circle of Sovereignty*, 62–64; also Exod 7:13; Deut 4:34; 6:22; 13:1–2; Isa 8:13; 20:3.

10 See further Longman, *Daniel*, 123, 126–28; Fewell, *Circle of Sovereignty*, 75–76; and Goldingay, *Daniel*, 89–90.

11 See further Fewell, *Circle of Sovereignty*, 81, 84–95; also Goldingay, *Daniel*, 113.

12 See further Longman, *Daniel*, 137.

13 Longman, 138.

sages are unable to interpret the message. The queen mother, probably Nebuchadnezzar's widow, reminds Belshazzar of Daniel, who was qualified to interpret the message because he "has the spirit of the holy gods in him" (Dan 5:11).

Daniel appears and explains the message—that Belshazzar has been weighed and found wanting by the Most High God. Daniel then announces the end of Belshazzar's reign, his impending death, and the emergence of the Medo-Persian Empire. As he begins to address the king, Daniel reminds Belshazzar that "the Most High God" gave Nebuchadnezzar "sovereignty and greatness and glory and splendor" (Dan 5:18). God is the one who has allowed both King Nebuchadnezzar and Belshazzar the power to rule, and "the Most High God is sovereign over all kingdoms on earth" (Dan 5:21).

Goldingay observes the irony that this pronouncement comes from the mouth of a Judean exile. The God of the Jewish exiles, whom Belshazzar has blasphemed, is more powerful than the Babylonian king.[14] Daniel conveys the message of his God to the king: "God has numbered the days of your reign and brought it to an end" (Dan 5:26). Punishing the king for his pride, blasphemy, and idolatry, God ends Belshazzar's life and allows Darius the Mede to take over the kingdom.[15]

Shadrach, Meshach, and Abednego, and the Fiery Furnace

In a fourth account of power in Daniel (Dan 3), Daniel's three companions are miraculously saved from a fiery furnace. Aiming to assert his power, Nebuchadnezzar crafts a gold image and orders everyone in Babylon to bow down to it. While scholars have debated whether this was an image of the king, something he had built, or a Babylonian god, the image does seem inspired by his dream in Daniel 2 in which his kingdom is symbolized by gold.[16] In any case, Fewell notes, "to worship the image is to swear allegiance to Nebuchadnezzar."[17]

A group of Babylonian court officials who detested the Judean exiles informs the king that Shadrach, Meshach, and Abednego have defied the order. When confronted by Nebuchadnezzar, the three men calmly communicate their resolve and trust in God's power.[18] Furious at their disobedience, the king orders the blazing furnace to be heated

---

14 See further Goldingay, *Daniel*, 114, 117.

15 See further Longman, *Daniel*, 145–46.

16 See further Longman, 97–98; also Fewell, *Circle of Sovereignty*, 38–39.

17 Fewell, *Circle of Sovereignty*, 40.

18 See further Fewell, 49–50.

seven times hotter than normal and commands that Shadrach, Meshach, and Abednego are bound with ropes and thrown into it. The intensity of the blaze actually kills the soldiers tasked with placing them in the fire. Fewell comments, "The executioners die meaningless deaths in obedience to an unconcerned sovereign with limited power."[19]

As the narrative continues, we see that the men's bodies would not burn, and they are miraculously saved: "The fire had not harmed their bodies, nor was a hair of their heads singed; their robes were not scorched, and there was no smell of fire on them" (Dan 3:27). Longman adds, "In this way, God is showing Nebuchadnezzar who is in charge."[20] Nebuchadnezzar recognizes a fourth person in the fire with the men—one who looked like "a son of the gods" (Dan 3:25). Later, the king calls this person an angel (Dan 3:28).[21] Likening the fourth person to "the angel of the LORD [who] encamps around those who fear him, and he delivers them" (Ps 34:7), Goldingay describes the fourth person as "the divine aide who camps round those who honor God and extricates them from peril … [and who] enters the fire himself to neutralize its capacity for harm by the presence of his superior energy."[22] Goldingay interprets this miraculous event in light of the resurrection of believers. God, who raises those who trust in him to new and eternal life, will also rescue them from death as well.[23]

In response to this miracle, Nebuchadnezzar recognizes the power of Shadrach, Meshach, and Abednego's God. Calling them out of the fire, he addresses them as "servants of the Most High God" (Dan 3:26). He not only praises them for their faith, but he also offers his own homage to the God of Israel:

> *Praise be to the God of Shadrach, Meshach and Abednego, who has sent his angel and rescued his servants! They trusted in him and defied the king's command and were willing to give up their lives rather than serve or worship any god except their own God." (Dan 3:28)*

King Nebuchadnezzar concludes with a decree quite different from the one at the outset of this account:

---

19 Fewell, 53.
20 Longman, *Daniel*, 102.
21 See further Longman, 103.
22 Goldingay, *Daniel*, 76.
23 See further Goldingay, 76.

> Therefore I decree that the people of any nation or language who say anything against the God of Shadrach, Meshach and Abednego be cut into pieces and their houses be turned into piles of rubble, for no other god can save in this way. (Dan 3:29)

Daniel in the Lions' Den

In another act of miraculous deliverance, Daniel's life is spared when he is thrown into a den of lions. Some of the ministers serving under the Persian King Darius had convinced the king to issue a temporary decree forbidding anyone to pray to any god except for the king for a period of thirty days (Dan 6:6–7). Jealous of Daniel's place of power in the kingdom, the ministers manipulated the king into signing this odd decree in order to entrap Daniel, who would surely refuse to cease his habit of praying to his God three times a day.[24] Since the edict was binding, Daniel was effectively sentenced to death by being thrown into a den of lions.

Though realizing he had been tricked, Darius acknowledges that the written law trumped his authority as king. Closing up the lions' den with the seal of his authority, Darius can only convey best wishes to Daniel: "May your God, whom you serve continually, rescue you!" (Dan 6:16). Longman notes that in the ancient world Daniel's situation was known as an "ordeal": a person is tortured, but if they survive, they emerge as the winner.[25] In this case, God makes Daniel victorious in the ordeal, and Daniel declares, "My God sent his angel, and he shut the mouths of the lions" (Dan 6:22). In preserving Daniel's life, God shows that he is more powerful than both King Darius and the laws of the Medo-Persians.[26]

Once Darius learns that Daniel has been spared, he also praises the God of Israel and emphasizes God's power:

> For he is the living God
> > and he endures forever;
> his kingdom will not be destroyed,
> > his dominion will never end.
> He rescues and he saves;
> > he performs signs and wonders
> > in the heavens and on the earth.
> He has rescued Daniel
> > from the power of the lions. (Dan 6:26–27)

---

24 See further Longman, *Daniel*, 160; also Fewell, *Circle of Sovereignty*, 107.
25 See further Longman, 163.
26 See further Longman, 158, 168.

In particular, Darius calls Daniel's God the "living God," which indicates God's "activity and power" in the affairs of this world.[27]

In summarizing the theme of power in Daniel, three observations can be made. First, in following the theme of Daniel—"the Most High is sovereign over all kingdoms on earth" (Dan 4:17)—God is directly behind the mighty acts of power. Through writing on the wall at Belshazzar's banquet, delivering Shadrach, Meshach, and Abednego from the fiery furnace, and protecting Daniel from the mouths of lions, God shows his authority over those in power—administrators, prime ministers, and kings. Fewell summarizes: "With the signs and wonders God brings down the mighty and delivers the troubled."[28]

Second, Daniel possesses God-given spiritual gifts to interpret Nebuchadnezzar's dreams and make sense of the handwriting on Belshazzar's banquet wall. Daniel had, of course, been trained as a Babylonian sage and had excelled with his natural abilities; however, Daniel distinguishes himself from his fellow sages through his God-given power. As shown, Nebuchadnezzar and the queen mother recognize that Daniel possesses the "spirit of the holy gods" (Dan 4:8–9; 5:11), or the "spirit of the gods" (Dan 5:14). While Almighty God was behind Daniel's miraculous works, Daniel also stewards these spiritual gifts to show God's power and bring glory to him.

> *God shows his authority over those in power—administrators, prime ministers, and kings.*

Finally, in the book of Daniel we observe specific accounts of spiritual warfare. While we see God demonstrating his power over kings and political leaders, we also see the kingdom of God clashing with unseen, spiritual forces in the world. Though not as apparent in the first six narrative chapters, spiritual warfare is demonstrated in Daniel's intercessory prayer in chapter 10, when Daniel learns that an angel has been delayed for three weeks while battling "the prince of the Persian kingdom" (Dan 10:13). This "prince" was some sort of demonic spirit that exercised spiritual control over the region. In the book of Daniel, God's power is at work in both the seen and unseen realms.

---

27 Goldingay, *Daniel*, 133; see also Longman, *Daniel*, 164.
28 Fewell, *Circle of Sovereignty*, 132.

God's Power for Mission in Scripture

God's Power in Israel

Daniel isn't the only person through whom God demonstrated his power in a missional way. This pattern continues throughout the Old Testament, particularly through Israel's story. During the Exodus (Exod 3–18), God miraculously parted the waters of the sea and delivered his people from slavery. On one hand, Israel was the mission field. Rescuing them through his power, the Lord fulfilled his purpose: "I will take you as my own people, and I will be your God. Then you will know that I am the LORD your God, who brought you out from under the yoke of the Egyptians" (Exod 6:7).[29]

On the other hand, through his mighty acts toward Israel, God also revealed himself to the Egyptians. Each of the plagues (Exod 7–11) specifically showed God's power over the gods of Egypt. In the final plague, many Egyptian families, including Pharaoh's house, lost their firstborn son when the angel of death passed over. However, Israelite families were spared because they sacrificed a lamb and placed the blood on their doorposts (Exod 12:1–30). Interestingly, during the Exodus the Israelites were joined by "a mixed multitude" (Exod 12:38 ESV)—Egyptians who put their faith in Israel's God and departed Egypt with them.

Because of the Exodus, God's fame spread further among the surrounding nations. In Moses and Miriam's song, they declared, "The chiefs of Edom will be terrified, the leaders of Moab will be seized with trembling, the people of Canaan will melt away" (Exod 15:15). More than mere poetry, these declarations are supported by the reaction of the inhabitants of Jericho to Israel's story. Speaking on behalf of the people of her city, Rahab, the prostitute who welcomed the Hebrew spies, stated:

> *I know that the LORD has given you this land and that a great fear of you has fallen on us, so that all who live in this country are melting in fear because of you. We have heard how the LORD dried up the water of the Red Sea for you when you came out of Egypt, and what you did to Sihon and Og, the two kings of the Amorites east of the Jordan, whom you completely destroyed. When we heard of it, our hearts melted in fear and everyone's courage failed because of you, for the LORD your God is God in heaven above and on the earth below. (Josh 2:9–11)*

---

29 See further Glasser, *Announcing the Kingdom*, 120.

The residents of Jericho, of course, experienced God's power firsthand when the Israelites conquered their city on the way to occupying the land of promise (Josh 5:13–6:27).

As Israel intermingled with the nations of the ancient Near East through warfare, commerce, and migration, many citizens of these nations came to see that Israel's God was the only true God. They affirmed, with Moses and Miriam, "Who among the gods is like you, LORD?" (Exod 15:11).[30]

When the Philistine champion Goliath taunted Israel's army, and young David in particular, David proclaimed, "You come against me with sword and spear and javelin, but I come against you in the name of the LORD Almighty" (1 Sam 17:45). David further explained his motivations for fighting Goliath and demonstrating God's power to the Philistines—that the "whole world will know that there is a God in Israel" (1 Sam 17:46).

Though Naaman was a commander of the Syrian army, which had fought against Israel, he came to Israel to seek healing for his leprosy. After dipping himself seven times in the Jordan River, at Elisha's direction, Naaman was miraculously healed. Having experienced God's power, he expressed to Elisha his belief in Israel's God: "Now I know that there is no God in all the world except in Israel" (2 Kgs 5:15).

God's greatness and power were some of the resounding themes that Israel sang about in the Psalms. In the salvation-history psalms (Pss 78, 105, 106), Israel remembers God's mighty acts of deliverance and the sovereign way in which he fashioned them into a nation, even amid their disobedience. For example, in Psalm 78, the psalmist declares:

> *He divided the sea and led them through;*
> > *he made the water stand up like a wall. ...*
>
> *he displayed his signs in Egypt,*
> > *his wonders in the region of Zoan. ...*
>
> *He drove out nations before them*
> > *and allotted their lands to them as an inheritance.* (Ps 78:13, 43, 55)

Many psalms, such as Psalm 22, declare the sovereignty of the God of Israel over the nations of the earth:

> *All the ends of the earth*
> > *will remember and turn to the Lord,*
>
> *and all the families of the nations*
> > *will bow down before him,*
>
> *for dominion belongs to the Lord*
> > *and he rules over the nations.* (Ps 22:27–28)[31]

---

30 See further 2 Sam 7:22; 1 Kgs 8:23,60; Isa 46:9.
31 See also Pss 19:4; 47:8; 82:8; 97:6.

The psalms further show God's sovereignty over the kings and political rulers of this world. Psalm 2 states: "Therefore, you kings, be wise; be warned, you rulers of the earth. Serve the LORD with fear and celebrate his rule with trembling" (Ps 2:10–11). Making a connection between the kings in Daniel to Psalm 2, Goldingay summarizes: "Heathen rulers have mustered and devised their plot, but God has acted on behalf of his servant, giving him the power to have them torn to pieces, to rule over their realm, and to compel them to serve God with trembling fear."[32]

Finally, other psalms, such as Psalm 86, proclaim God's power over other gods: "Among the gods there is none like you, Lord; no deeds can compare with yours" (Ps 86:8). In Psalm 96, the psalmist announces that the gods of this world are not really gods at all: "For all the gods of the nations are idols, but the LORD made the heavens" (Ps 96:5).

Power in the Ministry of Jesus

While preaching the kingdom of God, Jesus demonstrated power in his earthly ministry through performing signs and wonders. First, Jesus defied natural law by performing miracles. While a guest at a wedding banquet in Cana (John 2:1–11), Jesus prolonged the party by changing water into wine—"the first of the signs through which he revealed his glory; and his disciples believed in him" (John 2:11).

Second, Jesus healed the sick and the afflicted. Early in his ministry, our Lord encountered a man at the pool of Bethesda who had been lame for thirty-eight years. With authority, Jesus said to him, "Get up! Pick up your mat and walk" (John 5:8). His healing causes a stir in the community since it occurred on the Sabbath, and the man testifies to the Jewish religious leaders that Jesus had healed him.

Near the end of his life and ministry, Jesus passed through Jericho, where he met a blind man. In response to the man's petition, "Lord, I want to see," Jesus said to him, "Receive your sight; your faith has healed you." Luke then adds, "Immediately he received his sight and followed Jesus, praising God. When all the people saw it, they also praised God" (Luke 18:41–43).

Third, Jesus demonstrated God's power by delivering those oppressed by demons. In the Gentile region of the Gerasenes, Jesus meets a man controlled by an "impure spirit" (Mark 5:2). In a power encounter, Jesus commands the demons to come out of the man and sends them into a herd of pigs. Once delivered, the man believes in Jesus and pledges to follow

---

32 Goldingay, *Daniel*, 136.

> *While preaching the kingdom of God, Jesus demonstrated power in his earthly ministry through performing signs and wonders.*

him, but Jesus sends him back to his hometown. Mark writes: "So the man went away and began to tell in the Decapolis how much Jesus had done for him. And all the people were amazed" (Mark 5:20).

These representative examples of Jesus's ministry of miracles, healing, and deliverance display that Jesus's ministry was characterized not just by power but also by care for the whole person—their spiritual, physical, and emotional needs. This approach is consistent with how Jesus describes his own call to mission in Luke's Gospel: "The Spirit of the Lord is on me, because he has anointed me to proclaim good news to the poor. He has sent me to proclaim freedom for the prisoners and recovery of sight for the blind, to set the oppressed free, to proclaim the year of the Lord's favor" (Luke 4:18–19).

Jesus's greatest work—his death, burial, and resurrection—was also a work of God's power. At the cross, Christ not only paid the penalty for sins, but he also destroyed the works of the devil.[33] Paul writes, "And having disarmed the power and authorities, he made a public spectacle of them, triumphing over them by the cross" (Col 2:15). Paul adds that following Christ's crucifixion, our Lord was "appointed the Son of God in power by his resurrection from the dead" (Rom 1:4). Through the Father's power, Christ is raised from the dead and conquers death for himself and for all who believe in him.[34] Because of this, the church declares in the Apostles Creed, "I believe in ... the resurrection of the body, and the life everlasting."

Power in the New Testament Church

The New Testament church was birthed in power by the Holy Spirit on the Day of Pentecost. Luke writes:

> *Suddenly a sound like the blowing of a violent wind came from heaven and filled the whole house where they were sitting. They saw what seemed to be tongues of fire that separated and came to rest on each of them. All of them were filled with the Holy Spirit and began to speak in other tongues as the Spirit enabled them. (Acts 2:2–4)*

---

33 See further Isa 53:6; 1 Pet 2:24; Heb 2:14; 1 John 3:8.

34 See further Acts 2:24, 32; 3:15, 26; 4:10; 5:30; 10:40; 13:30–37; Rom 4:24; 6:4; 10:9; 1 Cor 6:14; Gal 1:1; Heb 2:14.

The assembled Jews are amazed by this outpouring of God's Spirit on the apostles. In a reversal of the Tower of Babel narrative (Gen 10–11), Jewish worshipers from many nations hear the gospel in their own language. Listening to Peter's anointed sermon from the texts of Joel and the Psalms, the assembled crowd inquires,

> "Brothers, what shall we do?
>
> Peter replied, "Repent and be baptized, every one of you, in the name of Jesus Christ for the forgiveness of your sins. And you will receive the gift of the Holy Spirit." (Acts 2:37–38)

Luke adds that because of the Holy Spirit's powerful, convicting work, "Those who accepted his message were baptized, and about three thousand were added to their number that day" (Acts 2:41).

Through the Apostle Paul's missionary church-planting work, the church expanded toward the ends of the earth. This ministry was also characterized by God's power. In Philippi (Acts 16:16–40), Paul and Silas were thrown into jail after delivering a fortune-telling slave girl from demonic oppression. As they sang hymns in prison, an earthquake erupted, breaking open the doors. Remaining in the prison and convincing the jailer not to take his own life, Paul and Silas go to his home, where their wounds are cared for and they are shown hospitality. Through this encounter, the jailer and his family came to believe the gospel.

Similar to the spiritual warfare that Daniel observes when the angel battles with the prince of Persia (Dan 10), Paul also recognizes the spiritual battle that accompanies his missionary work.

> For our struggle is not against flesh and blood, but against the rulers, against the authorities, against the powers of this dark world and against the spiritual forces of evil in the heavenly realms. Therefore put on the full armor of God, so that when the day of evil comes, you may be able to stand your ground, and after you have done everything, to stand. (Eph 6:12–13)

Paul acknowledges the existence of the evil one and that there was an ongoing cosmic spiritual battle between the kingdom of darkness and God's kingdom. Believers are involved in this battle and may be victorious through prayer and meditating on the Word of God. As Daniel experienced and testified, Paul shows that God is sovereign over all spiritual powers of darkness.

God's Power in Mission History

While the Old and New Testament Scriptures reveal a God of power in the work of mission, mission history also testifies to miracles, healings, and power encounters that accompany the spread of the gospel. We explore several examples here from the early, medieval, and modern church period.

Gregory Thaumaturgus (Asia Minor)

While a student in Palestinian Caesarea, Gregory Thaumaturgus (ca. 213–270) was led to faith in Christ by his professor, Origen of Alexandria (ca. 184–ca. 253). After returning home to Neo-Caesarea in Pontus, Gregory was ordained a bishop in 240. In addition to his duties as bishop, Gregory served as a committed evangelist. A gifted thinker, he put his training in philosophy, mathematics, and law to work in regular witness among pagan intellectuals.

Perhaps surprisingly, Gregory is also remembered for having a ministry of prayer, healing, and exorcising demons, particularly among the poor. Commenting on the impact of Gregory's ministry, Bishop Basil of Caesarea (ca. 329–ca. 379) stated with some intended hyperbole that when Gregory arrived in Pontus there were only seventeen Christians, but when he died, there were only seventeen nonbelievers.[35] Gregory's ministry of healing and deliverance surely contributed to the expansion of the gospel in Pontus.

Gregory the Illuminator (Armenia)

The Armenian historian Agathangelos reported that Gregory the Illuminator (ca. 240–332) came from Asia Minor in the late third century to serve the Armenian king. Because of his refusal to make sacrifices to the Armenian gods and because his father was an enemy of the Armenian King Trdat (r. 287–330), Gregory was tortured and thrown in prison for thirteen years. When Trdat and his family were afflicted by demons and became gravely ill, they summoned Gregory to pray for them. Healed from sickness and freed from demonic oppression, Trdat embraced the gospel and was baptized along with his household and the Armenian nobility.

The king also granted Gregory freedom to preach the gospel throughout his kingdom. In 301, Trdat took it a step farther and declared Christianity the national religion of Armenia, making it the first "Christian nation" in world history. Though this final turn of events is troubling for many students of

---

35 Basil, *On the Holy Spirit*, 74; Basil, *Letter* 28, *Letters*.

> *Healed from sickness and freed from demonic oppression, Trdat embraced the gospel and was baptized along with his household and the Armenian nobility.*

mission history, it does not take away from Gregory's meaningful witness that was accompanied by power.

Boniface (Germany)

During the eighth century, the English monk Boniface (ca. 680–754) served as a missionary bishop among Germanic peoples in northern Europe. Boniface is best remembered for a power encounter that occurred earlier in his ministry among the Frisian people. He confronted the Frisians' pagan religion head-on when he cut down the sacred oak tree of Thor in the town of Geismar. His biographer wrote:

> Boniface in their presence attempted to cut down, at a place called Geismar, a certain oak of extraordinary size called in the old tongue of the pagans the Oak of [Thor]. Taking his courage in his hands (for a great crowd of pagans stood by watching and bitterly cursing in their hearts the enemy of the gods), he cut the first notch. But when he had made a superficial cut, suddenly, the oak's vast bulk, shaken by a mighty blast of wind from above crashed to the ground shivering its topmost branches into fragments in its fall. As if by the express will of God (for the brethren present had done nothing to cause it) the oak burst asunder into four parts, each part having a trunk of equal length. At the sight of this extraordinary spectacle the heathens who had been cursing ceased to revile and began, on the contrary, to believe and bless the Lord. Thereupon the holy bishop took counsel with the brethren, built an oratory from the timber of the oak and dedicated it to Saint Peter the Apostle.[36]

Though Boniface enjoyed a certain measure of protection from the Frankish kings and military, which may have encouraged his actions at Geismar, he ultimately died as a martyr in 754 while preaching the gospel to the Frisians. Though Boniface was committed to preaching, making disciples, and establishing new churches, the pagan Frisians seemed to respond to the gospel in part because of the demonstration of divine power at Geismar.[37]

---

36 Talbot, *Life of Boniface*, 6.
37 See further Smither, *Missionary Monks*, 93–106.

William Wadé Harris (West Africa)

Originally part of the Methodist and Episcopal churches in Liberia, William Wadé Harris (ca. 1860–1929) served as an itinerant prophet-evangelist in his home region of West Africa. From 1914 to 1929, Harris preached between Liberia and Ivory Coast, baptizing as many as one hundred thousand West Africans. His message included a call for his fellow Africans to abandon fetishes and idols.

Harris also valued the visible work of the Holy Spirit. Observers reported that his message was accompanied by miracles, healing, and speaking in tongues. Harris' ministry also set the stage for the development of African independent churches—church movements that were not connected to Western denominations. Often Pentecostal in doctrine, these churches were also culturally African in worship forms.[38]

During the twentieth century, most of the church growth in the African context happened through the ministry of African believers. Through a ministry of preaching accompanied by power encounters, Harris contributed significantly to African mission.

Waodoni Mission (Ecuador)

The mission to the Waodoni (sometimes spelled Waorani or Huaorani) people in 1955 and 1956 serves as one of the most famous missionary martyr stories for the Western church in the twentieth century. Five young American men (Jim Elliot, Nate Saint, Pete Fleming, Roger Youderian, and Ed McCully) and their wives strived to make peaceful contact with and evangelize a Stone Age tribe in the Ecuadorian jungle. Since their previous contact with outsiders had only been violent, the Waodoni people were known as the Aucas ("savages").

Living among a nearby tribe and learning some of the Waodoni language, the men initiated friendly contact with the Waodoni. Eventually, they set up a meeting with some of the tribesmen. After landing on a beach alongside the Curaray River in Waodoni territory on January 8, 1956, the men prayed, sang a hymn, and went to meet the Waodoni. Tragedy followed. The five men were massacred by the Waodoni tribesmen, who believed them to be cannibals.

Despite these tragic murders, Elisabeth Eliot (Jim Eliot's wife) and Rachel Saint (Nate Saint's sister) later made peaceful contact with the Waodoni, accepted an invitation to live among them, and helped plant a church among the tribal people. One of the Waodoni men who speared

---

38 See Shenk, "Legacy of William Wadé Harris," 170–76.

> *Worship and power played a significant role in this account of missionary martyrdom.*

the Americans on the beach believed the gospel and became a pastor in the Waodoni church and a missionary to neighboring tribes in Ecuador.[39]

Worship and power played a significant role in this account of missionary martyrdom. The five men worshiped and sang hymns before meeting the Waodoni. However, years later, the Waodoni tribesmen also talked about hearing worship—something like a choir of angels singing around them—after the men had died. They apparently experienced a power encounter in which they were enveloped in worship—an experience that seemed instrumental in their becoming open to the missionaries' God and believing the gospel.[40]

God's Power in Contemporary Mission

Though we live in an increasingly secular Western world where supernatural claims are met with skepticism, God still seems pleased to accomplish his mission through the church through acts of power. This seems particularly evident with gospel witness among Muslims.

I have a friend who served for many years as a pastor of a church in a predominantly Muslim country in the Middle East. During the 1980s, when his nation was at war with a neighboring country, it was not unusual for his city to be attacked with bombs and missiles. Air-raid sirens sounded constantly, warning the local population to take cover.

One day a missile ripped through the roof of the pastor's church building and landed behind his pulpit, but it did not detonate. The word quickly spread that God was protecting the Christians. After that incident, whenever the siren sounded, the church filled up with Muslims seeking that same protection. Whenever my friend heard the air-raid siren, he would drive to the church and begin preaching the gospel to these visitors.

On another occasion, the youth in the same church, who were getting excited about their faith, came to the pastor asking about ways to serve. Because there were many people out in the villages and rural areas without access to Scripture, he sent them on a trip to distribute Bibles. While on their journey, the steering wheel of their vehicle locked up, and the driver

---

39 See further Elliot, *Shadow of the Almighty*; and Elliot, *Through Gates of Splendor*.
40 See further Liefield, *Unfolding Destinies*.

barely got the car off the road. When the car stopped, they met a man standing under a tree.

The man, who was from a local village, asked, "Do you have my Bible?" Surprised, the youth asked why he was requesting a Bible.

"Last night, Jesus appeared to me in my village and said, 'read my Word.' I told him we did not have his Word, and he said to come here and wait. And you're the first people who have come by today."

The youth were amazed at this clear and powerful act of God to lead this man to the Scriptures and the gospel!

Many Muslims who have come to faith in Christ have reported a dream encounter with the Lord. Because this phenomenon has become so prevalent, one ministry center in Europe that produces gospel programs on air and online now keeps track of their listeners and correspondents who report dreams about God.

> *Many Muslims who have come to faith in Christ have reported a dream encounter with the Lord.*

In my own journey, living in North Africa and Europe, several Muslim friends came to me and shared such dream experiences. For many of these friends, this powerful experience (and the deep conviction of sin that accompanied it) was instrumental in their conversion to faith in Christ.

Summary: God's Power in Mission Today

As I asserted at the beginning of this chapter, one of the greatest desires of people in the world is to have power. Driven by fear of evil spirits, curses, physical illnesses, and abandonment, and desiring solutions for daily problems (money, work, relationship challenges), people crave power over their lives. Commenting on religious practices in folk, or popular, Islam, including rituals and sacrifices that aren't taught in the official faith, Dudley Woodberry notes, "The felt need for power is so great among folk Muslims that their entire worldview is seen through the spectacles of power."[41]

While the concern for power is strongly supported in missiological, anthropological, and folk-religion literature, the worldview of Christians, particularly those from the West, can still be quite secular. In his 1983 groundbreaking article, "The Flaw of the Excluded Middle," Paul Hiebert identified the dualistic worldview of many Christians: (1) a religious

---
41 Cited in Love, *Muslims, Magic, and the Kingdom of God*, 1.

worldview that addresses ultimate, otherworldly questions and (2) a scientific worldview that proposes rational explanations for present-world matters. As a result, Hiebert argued that an "excluded middle" emerges, one which has no explanation for the spiritual, demonic, or magical realm in the present world.[42] Commenting on this reality in a folk Muslim context, Rick Love adds:

> *Since most western missionaries come from a materialistic-oriented culture which relegates the supernatural to other-worldly concerns, when faced with the realities of the spirit realm, they often either ignore the issues or offer naturalistic solutions to what are perceived by Folk Muslims as supernaturally-caused problems—so opportunities for ministry are lost.*[43]

While some time has passed since Hiebert, Love, and others raised these questions, Western Christians still struggle to find a place in their theology for the spirit world. In 2020, Haitian missiologist Patrick Gue asserted that Haitian Wesleyans have yet to cultivate a theology of power because of the prevailing influence of Western missionaries on the island. Haitian believers attend church, read the Bible, and pray; but many will also consult voodoo practitioners when they face economic, health, or spiritual problems.[44]

Excluded-middle theology has also developed because of some forms of cessationism—the belief that miracles, healing, deliverance, and spiritual gifts such as tongues ceased with the death of the original apostles. Believing that such acts of power were assigned to an age of miracles, missionaries trained in this theological tradition have had little to offer to global peoples struggling with spiritual warfare and other conflicts.

Proposing an evangelical theology of power, Hiebert calls for a holistic approach to mission. Missionaries working among folk Muslims should affirm God's presence and care for their new friends' daily needs, share the availability of God's power for their lives, and encourage their friends to call upon the Lord for physical healing and deliverance from evil spirits.[45] With the growth of the church in the Global South in the twentieth and twenty-first centuries, their leaders have proposed a theology of power for the global church, challenging the flaw of the excluded middle.

---

42 See further Hiebert, "Flaw of the Excluded Middle," 146–58.
43 Love, *Muslims, Magic, and Kingdom of God*, 6.
44 See further Gue, "Toward a Haitian."
45 See further Hiebert, "Power Encounter and Folk Islam," 54–60.

In January of 1978, the Lausanne Committee's Theology and Education Group convened a consultation on "Gospel and Culture." This group of theologians, missiologists, pastors, and missionaries affirmed:

> *A number of us, especially those from Asia, Africa, and Latin America, have spoken both of the reality of evil powers and of the necessity to demonstrate the supremacy of Jesus over them. For conversion involves a power encounter. People give their allegiance to Christ when they see that his power is superior to magic and voodoo, the curses and blessings of witch doctors, and the malevolence of evil spirits, and that his salvation is a real liberation from the power of evil and death.*
>
> *Of course, some are questioning today whether a belief in spirits is compatible with our modern scientific understanding of the universe. We wish to affirm, therefore, against the mechanistic myth on which the typical Western world-view rests, the reality of demonic intelligences which are concerned by all means, overt and covert, to discredit Jesus Christ and keep people from coming to him. We think it vital in evangelism in all cultures to teach the reality and hostility of demonic powers, and to proclaim that God has exalted Christ as Lord of all and that Christ, who really does possess all power, however we may fail to acknowledge this, can (as we proclaim him) break through any world-view in any mind to make his lordship known and bring about a radical change of heart and outlook.*[46]

Relating this theology of power to conversion, Charles Kraft describes two types of encounters: power encounters, which "release people from satanic captivity and bring them into freedom in Jesus Christ," and truth encounters, which "counter error and ... bring people to correct understandings about Jesus Christ."[47]

The church today can emphasize mission in power in a few tangible and sober ways. First, we can adopt the habit of praying the Lord's Prayer daily. While we can pray the prayer itself from start to finish, we can also use the seven petitions in the prayer as a framework and launching point for spontaneous prayers. In particular, when we pray "Your kingdom come," we are praying that the reign of Christ will come to bear in our present world—that God will bring justice, peace, healing, and liberation. Related, "Deliver us from evil" is a petition of spiritual warfare. We pray for

---

46 "The Willowbank Report," Lausanne Occasional Paper.
47 Kraft, "What Kind of Encounters Do We Need?" 258–67.

God's victory over and deliverance from the evil one—his demons, or evil spirits. In praying this, global Christians may experience God's power over spiritual darkness, and they will resist the urge to turn to other promises of power (i.e., voodoo, magic, fortune-tellers).

Second, we ought to pray for healing for the sick and suffering around us. In reality, this is not a new thing, as the Scriptures admonish us to pray for the sick. James writes:

> *Is anyone among you sick? Let them call the elders of the church to pray over them and anoint them with oil in the name of the Lord. And the prayer offered in faith will make the sick person well; the Lord will raise them up. If they have sinned, they will be forgiven. (Jas 5:14–15)*

The Anglican Church applies this teaching very specifically through a series of healing services and prayers for the sick. In "Ministry to the Sick," a rite within *The Book of Common Prayer*, the minister prays:

> *N., [person's name] I anoint you with oil and I lay my hands upon you in the Name of the Father, and of the Son, and of the Holy Spirit. Amen.*
>
> *Lord Jesus Christ, heal this your servant, sustain him with your presence, drive away all sickness of body, mind, and spirit, and give to him that victory of life and peace which will enable him to serve you both now and evermore. Amen.*[48]

Finally, we ought to pray for those who are oppressed by evil spirits. This presents a great opportunity to follow the pattern of the Lord's Prayer and pray, "Deliver us from evil." From the early church period, many church leaders and believers have engaged in spiritual warfare, praying through the practice of exorcism. While church fathers such as Ambrose of Milan (ca. 340–397) practiced exorcism throughout his ministry and included trained exorcists on his pastoral team, early church baptismal liturgies also included a call for renunciation.[49]

Candidates for baptism were asked to embrace Christ as Lord and to renounce the works of Satan in their flesh. Even today, the baptismal liturgy in *The Book of Common Prayer* contains these promises in the profession of faith:

---

48 *The Book of Common Prayer*, 226.
49 See further Smither, *Augustine as Mentor*, 72–74.

> Question: Do you renounce the devil and all the spiritual forces of wickedness that rebel against God?
>
> Answer: I renounce them.[50]

Early and medieval Celtic Christians prayed prayers known as *loricas*—prayers for God to go before and behind them and to protect them from physical, human, and spiritual evil. A great example of this is the famous "Breastplate of St. Patrick," which includes these spiritual warfare petitions:

> *I rise today*
>
> *with the power of God to pilot me*
>
> *God's host to deliver me:*
>
> *—from the snares of devils,*
>
> *—from evil temptations,*
>
> *—from nature's failings,*
>
> *—from all who wish me harm ...*
>
> *Christ with me, Christ before me, Christ behind me;*
>
> *Christ within me, Christ beneath me, Christ above me;*
>
> *Christ to right of me, Christ to left of me;*
>
> *Christ in my lying, Christ in my sitting, Christ in my rising.*[51]

While the prayers of the early church reflected a keen awareness of the spiritual world, including attacks and temptations from the evil one, these prayers are not dramatic or sensational in tone. Instead, they are sober reflections—a faithful application of our Lord's admonition to pray, "Deliver us from evil."

Mission in the way of Daniel includes ministry in word and power. In word, we proclaim the death, burial, and resurrection of Christ and we make disciples of all peoples by teaching them to obey all that Christ has commanded. In power, we trust God to demonstrate his mighty acts through healing, deliverance, and other miracles. While we don't claim that God will heal or deliver in every situation, we do believe that God is able, and that in demonstrating his power, he will draw people from every cultural group to himself in saving faith.

---

50 *The Book of Common Prayer*, 164.

51 "Patrick's Breastplate," in *Celtic Spirituality*, 119–20.

Questions for Reflection

1. What does this chapter teach you about spiritual warfare and God's power for mission in Scripture?
2. How would you describe your worldview in regard to the spiritual world? Do you have an "excluded middle" in your view of the world?
3. What have you learned about the place of power in mission today?
4. After reading this chapter, how will your prayers and witness to others be different this week?

CHAPTER 5

Emboldened: Witness, Prayer, and Suffering

Educated in the language and culture of the Babylonians, trained as a sage, and promoted to government service, Daniel lived, worked, and witnessed in the public square of Babylonian and Persian society. Through his education and assimilation into these host cultures, Daniel became a culturally relevant witness.[1] This value of cultural relevance was reflected in the writing of Daniel's text: nearly half of it (2:4b to 7:28) was written in Aramaic, the vernacular of the Babylonians. While Jewish exiles could be encouraged by Daniel's testimony of the Most High God, the Babylonians and other surrounding nations could also learn of God's ways.

Daniel made his home in Babylon and sought the welfare and peace of his adopted land, but he and his companions still encountered prejudice, hardship, and suffering. Despite gaining favor throughout their careers in Babylon and Persia, they continued to be called "exiles from Judah" (Dan 2:25; 3:12; 5:13; 6:13). Shadrach, Meshach, and Abednego were thrown into the fiery furnace because of the testimony of jealous colleagues (Dan 3:8–12). Similarly, Daniel was targeted by

---
1 See further Longman, *Daniel*, 62–66.

other administrators in Persia because of his faith (Dan 6:5). Although these men ultimately survived the furnace and the lions' den because of God's mighty acts, we cannot diminish the stress and anguish they would have felt in the process. Reflecting on the struggles of Daniel and his friends ought to sober us to the painful reality of suffering and make us resist the temptation to romanticize such hardship.

Bold Witness

Amid prejudice, hardship, and suffering, Daniel and his companions maintained a bold witness for God. Their approach to witness was multifaceted, revealing a conviction to witness through their godly lives as well as their words. *First*, as we observed in the opening chapter of the book, Daniel and his companions demonstrated an allegiance to their God by not defiling themselves through eating the food from the king's table, as their fellow Jewish exiles were doing. While the young men were polite and found favor with the Babylonian officials, their bold witness did not come primarily through their actual words but through their actions as they preserved their integrity and remained faithful to their God.[2]

> *Daniel and his companions were bold witnesses by speaking truth to power*

Second, while Daniel demonstrated God's power through interpreting dreams and other acts of power, he verbally attributed this power to God. For example, before interpreting Nebuchadnezzar's first dream, Daniel declares: "No wise man, enchanter, magician or diviner can explain to the king the mystery he has asked about, but there is a God in heaven who reveals mysteries" (Dan 2:27–28). During the explanation of the dream, Daniel proclaims to the king that it is "the God of heaven" who had given Nebuchadnezzar "dominion and power and might and glory" (Dan 2:37), and that "the great God has shown the king what will take place in the future" (Dan 2:45).

Third, Daniel and his companions were bold witnesses by speaking truth to power. In interpreting Nebuchadnezzar's second dream, Daniel told the king that the Most High would drive him from his throne, cause him to lose his sanity, and send him to live among animals. Daniel adds that God's purpose was for Nebuchadnezzar to "acknowledge that the

---

2 See further Fewell, *Circle of Sovereignty*, 16–17.

Most High is sovereign over all kingdoms on earth and gives them to anyone he wishes" (Dan 4:25). Daniel continues his witness by actually calling the king to repent: "Renounce your sins by doing what is right, and your wickedness by being kind to the oppressed" (Dan 4:27).

Similarly, before explaining to King Belshazzar the meaning of the writing on the wall, Daniel refuses all gifts and privileges and condemns the king: "You have set yourself up against the Lord of heaven. ... You did not honor the God who holds in his hand your life and all your ways" (Dan 5:23). Interpreting the writing on the wall, he tells Belshazzar that he has been "weighed on the scales and found wanting" (Dan 5:27) by Almighty God, who is giving his kingdom to the Medo-Persians.[3]

In their refusal to bow down to Nebuchadnezzar's golden statue, Shadrach, Meshach, and Abednego also spoke truth to power. Most of the people in Nebuchadnezzar's realm would have had no problem obeying the king's order, since they were already polytheists. Going against this religious trend, the men refused the order because of their convictions as pious Jews that there was only one God worthy of worship. They remembered the first two of the Ten Commandments: "You shall have no other gods before me," and "You shall not make yourself an idol in the form of anything" (Exod 20:3-4).

While going against the grain of Babylonian polytheism, the men also broke with Israel's historic habit of worshiping idols—practices that had led to their destruction and conquest by the Babylonians in the first place. Not aiming to become martyrs, the three men initially refused the king's order quietly.[4]

After being accused by the other administrators and then summoned by the king, Shadrach, Meshach, and Abednego offer a bold verbal response. In a confrontational ceremony that begins with "the horn, flute, zither, lyre, harp, pipe and all kinds of music," Nebuchadnezzar orders them to "fall down and worship the image I made" (Dan 3:15)—a clear test of their loyalty as his subjects and government administrators.[5] The king adds: "But if you do not worship it, you will be thrown immediately into a blazing furnace. Then what god will be able to rescue you from my hand?" (Dan 3:15).

---

3 See further Longman, *Daniel*, 140–41.

4 See further Longman, 96, 104–8.

5 See further Longman, 100.

Refusing to comply, the men reply:

> *If we are thrown into the blazing furnace, the God we serve is able to deliver us from it, and he will deliver us from Your Majesty's hand. But even if he does not, we want you to know, Your Majesty, that we will not serve your gods or worship the image of gold you have set up." (Dan 3:17–18)*

Through this experience, the men convey two compelling ideas. First, their God is powerful and able to rescue them. Second, their allegiance to God is not contingent on whether or not he will save them.[6] Commenting on this passage in his classic work *Knowing God*, J. I. Packer writes that the men demonstrate the "spirit of all who know God. ... They may find the determination of the right course to be agonizingly difficult, but once they are clear on it, they embrace it boldly and without hesitation."[7]

Fourth, Daniel was a man of prayer who also witnessed to God through his commitment to prayer. As we've shown, when tasked with interpreting Nebuchadnezzar's first dream, Daniel went home and asked Shadrach, Meshach, and Abednego to pray (Dan 2:18). Later, we learn that "in prayer and petition, in fasting, and in sackcloth and ashes" (Dan 9:3), Daniel prayed prayers of confession and repentance on the part of sinful and displaced Judah.[8] During another period of fasting, prayer, and visions (Dan 10:1–21), Daniel engaged in spiritual-warfare praying that included angels and the demonic "prince of Persia."

When Daniel's prayer life became the focus of his colleagues' attempt to entrap him with the temporary decree to pray only to King Darius, Daniel witnessed through his habits of prayer. A pious Jewish exile, he opened his windows three times a day to pray in the direction of Jerusalem, where the temple had been destroyed (Dan 6:10, 13). Though praying three times a day is not prescribed in Scripture, the practice was affirmed by David: "Evening, morning, and noon I cry out in distress, and he hears my voice" (Ps 55:17).

While Daniel's prayers appear to be personal and private (he was not leading corporate prayers), they were by no means secret prayers. By opening his windows, he gave witness to his God through prayer.[9] Of course, Daniel's witness became more public and widespread when he

---

6 See further Longman, 101; and Fewell, *Circle of Sovereignty*, 49–50.

7 Packer, *Knowing God*, 26.

8 See further Fewell, *Circle of Sovereignty*, 122–23.

9 See further Longman, *Daniel*, 161; also Goldingay, *Daniel*, 128–29, 131–32.

was unjustly thrown into the lions' den and then miraculously saved from it by God's power.

Fifth, Daniel's witness included specific references to the Messiah. In interpreting Nebuchadnezzar's first dream, Daniel described a kingdom symbolized by a rock that "will never be destroyed" and that "will crush all those kingdoms and bring them to an end" (Dan 2:44–45). Throughout Scripture, this rock clearly points to the person of Christ. Pulling together teaching from Isaiah and the Psalms, Peter preaches that the "living Stone" is Christ:

> As you come to him, the living Stone—rejected by humans but chosen by God and precious to him—you also, like living stones, are being built into a spiritual house to be a holy priesthood, offering spiritual sacrifices acceptable to God through Jesus Christ. For in Scripture it says:
>
> "See, I lay a stone in Zion,
>   a chosen and precious cornerstone,
> and the one who trusts in him
>   will never be put to shame."
>
> Now to you who believe, this stone is precious. But to those who do not believe,
>
> "The stone the builders rejected
>   has become the cornerstone," and,
> "A stone that causes people to stumble
>   and a rock that makes them fall." (1 Pet 2:4–8a)[10]

Outside of the narrative chapters of Daniel's book, in which he engaged in direct witness, the prophet further testified to the Messiah. In a vision in chapter 7, Daniel sees "one like a son of man, coming with the clouds of heaven. ... He was given authority, glory and sovereign power; all nations and peoples of every language worshiped him" (Dan 7:13–14). Like the indestructible rock of Daniel 2, "his dominion is an everlasting dominion that will not pass away, and his kingdom is one that will never be destroyed" (Dan 7:14). In chapter 9, Daniel speaks of the coming of an "Anointed One" who "will be put to death" (Dan 9:26). The broader witness of Scripture indicates that in these descriptions Daniel is speaking of the person and work of Christ.[11]

---

10 See further Ps 118:22; Matt 21:42; Mark 12:10–11; Luke 20:17; Isa 8:14; 28:16; Rom 9:33; and Longman, *Daniel*, 92.

11 See further Goldingay, *Daniel*, 192–93, 267–68; also Longman, *Daniel*, 61.

The Witness of Kings

Finally, a fascinating aspect in the narrative chapters of Daniel was the witness of kings after they encountered Daniel's God. After interpreting Nebuchadnezzar's first dream, Daniel declares that this miracle was accomplished by God's power, and the king concurs: "Surely your God is the God of gods and the Lord of kings and a revealer of mysteries, for you were able to reveal this mystery" (Dan 2:47).

In Nebuchadnezzar's account of his second dream, he introduces and concludes the narrative with words of praise for Daniel's God. Addressing the "nations and peoples of every language, who live in all the earth" (Dan 4:1)—the diverse cultural groups in his Babylonian realm—the king writes:

> It is my pleasure to tell you about the miraculous signs and wonders that the Most High God has performed for me.
>
> How great are his signs,
>> how mighty his wonders!
>
> His kingdom is an eternal kingdom;
>> his dominion endures from generation to generation. (Dan 4:2–3) [12]

Nebuchadnezzar refers to God's actions as "signs and wonders," which resounds with God's mighty acts in the Old Testament.[13] Once his sanity is restored, Nebuchadnezzar concludes with his own doxology to Daniel's God:

> Then I praised the Most High; I honored and glorified him who lives forever.
>
> His dominion is an eternal dominion;
>> his kingdom endures from generation to generation. ...
>
> All the peoples of the earth
>> Are regarded as nothing.
>
> He does as he pleases
>> with the powers of heaven
>> and the peoples of the earth. (Dan 4:34–35)

---

12 See further Longman, 118.
13 See further Fewell, *Circle of Sovereignty*, 62–64; also Exod 7:13; Deut 4:34; 6:22; 13:1–2; Isa 8:13; 20:3.

In short, the Babylonian king acknowledges Daniel's God—the one true God who humbles proud leaders, such as Nebuchadnezzar.[14]

When Shadrach, Meshach, and Abednego emerge miraculously from the blazing furnace, Nebuchadnezzar declares:

> *Praise be to the God of Shadrach, Meshach and Abednego, who has sent his angel and rescued his servants! They trusted in him and defied the king's command and were willing to give up their lives rather than serve or worship any god except their own God. Therefore I decree that the people of any nation or language who say anything against the God of Shadrach, Meshach and Abednego be cut into pieces and their houses be turned into piles of rubble, for no other god can save in this way. (Dan 3:28–29)*

Ironically, at the outset of this narrative, the king orders the men to bow down to a statute he has erected; and by the end, he is exalting *their* God. He also goes from condemning them to death in a fiery furnace to threatening the lives of those who speak against the God of Israel.

Following God's mighty act of power in rescuing Daniel from the den of lions, Darius puts his thoughts about Daniel's God in a letter that he addresses to "all the nations and peoples of every language in all the earth" (Dan 6:25). He writes:

> *May you prosper greatly!*
>
> *I issue a decree that in every part of my kingdom people must fear and reverence the God of Daniel.*
>
> > *For he is the living God*
> > > *and he endures forever;*
> >
> > *his kingdom will not be destroyed,*
> > > *his dominion will never end.*
> >
> > *He rescues and he saves;*
> > > *he performs signs and wonders*
> > > *in the heavens and on the earth.*
> >
> > *He has rescued Daniel*
> > > *from the power of the lions. (Dan 6:25b–27)*

---

14 See further Longman, *Daniel*, 123, 126–28; Fewell, *Circle of Sovereignty*, 75–76; and Goldingay, *Daniel*, 89–90.

Similar to Nebuchadnezzar, Darius issues an initial decree calling his subjects to pray to him and then he issues a second one urging them to worship Daniel's God.[15]

Analyzing the statements, letters, and decrees from these ancient kings can be perplexing. In some respects, their words sound like the Psalms. They speak of God's power and authority, and like other authors in Scripture, they highlight his signs and wonders. That said, I don't think we can fully know what was in their hearts and if they indeed became believers in Israel's God. But in the very least, they experienced the Most High God's power and then testified about it to a vast group of peoples within their spheres of power. We can infer that much of the known world in ancient Babylon and Persia learned of God's ways, and some probably became worshipers of the God of Daniel.[16]

Bold Witness and Suffering in Mission in Scripture

Like Daniel and his companions, other figures in broader Scripture also demonstrated a bold witness amid suffering. They lived holy lives, attributed acts of power to God, and spoke truth to power. In this section, we focus on some representative examples in the New Testament and first-century church.

John the Baptist

Matthew, Mark, and Luke remember John the Baptizer as the fulfillment of Isaiah's prophecy: "A voice of one calling in the wilderness, 'Prepare the way for the Lord, make straight paths for him'" (Luke 3:4; Isa 40:3–5). A desert-dweller subsisting on an austere diet and wearing simple clothes, John experienced hardship that was self-imposed because of his ascetic lifestyle. He preached a confrontational message of repentance that probably didn't comfort the hearts of his listeners, yet many responded and received John's baptism of repentance.[17]

As a preaching prophet, John also spoke truth to power and denounced Herod's immoral ways. Luke writes: "But when John rebuked Herod the tetrarch because of his marriage to Herodias, his brother's wife, and all the other evil things he had done, Herod ... locked John up in prison" (Luke 3:19–20).

---

15 See further Longman, *Daniel*, 164.
16 See further Goldingay, *Daniel*, 129.
17 See also Matt 13:1–12; Mark 1:1–8.

After Herodias' daughter pleased Herod with a dance at his birthday celebration, Herodias took her revenge against John by convincing her daughter to request John's head as her reward (Mark 6:17–29). Reflecting on John's execution, Jesus also comments on the suffering and hardship that often accompanies preaching the gospel: "From the days of John the Baptist until now, the kingdom of heaven has been subjected to violence, and violent people have been raiding it" (Matt 11:12). John preached boldly, through hardship and suffering.

Jesus

Jesus's earthly ministry was also thoroughly shaped by hardship and suffering. The Gospel writers are clear in identifying the Lord as the Suffering Servant from Isaiah (Isa 52:13–53:12)—the one who endured God's wrath, took the punishment for sinners, physically suffered without any verbal defense, died, and was buried. Indeed, the passion of Christ was the pinnacle of his suffering and redemptive work. Jesus came to die for sinners.

Even before the cross, Jesus was a suffering witness in his sacred humanity. "Being in very nature God," and not considering "equality with God something to be used to his own advantage" (Phil 2:6), our Lord was humbled in the incarnation. Narrowly escaping genocide as a baby, Jesus and his family fled to Egypt as refugees. During his earthly ministry, Jesus encountered opposition from Jewish religious leaders and people in his hometown. After hearing Jesus's claims to be the Messiah in the synagogue in Nazareth, "All the people in the synagogue were furious. ... They got up, drove him out of the town, and took him to the brow of the hill on which the town was built, in order to throw him off the cliff. But he walked through the crowd and went on his way" (Luke 4:28–29).[18] Amid hardship, suffering, and death, Jesus boldly preached the kingdom of God.

> *Even before the cross, Jesus was a suffering witness in his sacred humanity.*

The Church in Acts

The first-century church in Acts boldly witnessed for Christ while sharing in his suffering.[19] In Jerusalem, the apostles were preaching and healing at

---

18 See further Smither, *Christian Martyrdom*, 1–9.
19 See further Sunquist, *Understanding Christian Mission*, 199–200.

Solomon's Colonnade (Acts 5:12–42), a ministry that got them arrested by the high priest and thrown into the public jail. During the night, an angel opened the doors of the jail and instructed the apostles to go back to the temple courts and continue preaching. Arrested again, they were brought back before the Sanhedrin and ordered to explain their actions. Similar to Shadrach, Meshach, and Abednego before Nebuchadnezzar, the apostles declared, "We must obey God rather than men" (Acts 5:29 ESV).

The Apostle Paul's call to Christ and to ministry included this promise from the Lord: "I will show him how much he must suffer for my name" (Acts 9:16). A survey of Paul's pioneer church-planting work through multiple missionary journeys in Acts reveals a pattern of hardship and suffering. When Paul describes his ministry, he speaks of sharing "abundantly in the sufferings of Christ" (2 Cor 1:5), filling up in his flesh "what is still lacking in regard to Christ's afflictions" (Col 1:24), and bearing on his body "the marks of Jesus" (Gal 6:17). He added that "for Christ's sake, I delight in weaknesses, in insults, in hardships, in persecutions, in difficulties. For when I am weak, then I am strong" (2 Cor 12:10).

In a concrete summary of his hardships in mission, specifically in comparison to the false apostles who were infiltrating the church at Corinth, Paul stated:

> *I have worked much harder, been in prison more frequently, been flogged more severely, and been exposed to death again and again. Five times I received from the Jews the forty lashes minus one. Three times I was beaten with rods, once I was pelted with stones, three times I was shipwrecked, I spent a night and a day in the open sea, I have been constantly on the move. I have been in danger from rivers, in danger from bandits, in danger from my fellow Jews, in danger from Gentiles; in danger in the city, in danger in the country, in danger at sea; and in danger from false believers. (2 Cor 11:23–26)*

According to church tradition, Paul was beheaded in Rome in AD 68, ending a remarkable journey of itinerant preaching, church planting, and suffering for the gospel.

Bold Witness and Suffering in Mission History

In the early, medieval, and even modern church period, the gospel continued to spread through those who endured hardship and suffering but maintained a bold witness. Dale Irvin and Scott Sunquist helpfully summarize: "The earliest Christian missionaries from Jerusalem went out as refugees and victims of persecution. ... These first Christians had expansionist tendencies without worldly power."[20]

Early North African Church

During the first three centuries, leading up to the conversion of Emperor Constantine in 312, the most rapid church growth in the Roman Empire took place in North Africa, in contexts of suffering. François Decret writes, "The opening pages of North African Christianity seem to have no connection with ... a great saint, or an apostle arriving on the African shores to convert the unbelievers. Rather this history opens through the testimonies of blood."[21]

Because many believers were put to death by lions or other wild beasts in the Carthage amphitheater, North African Christians cultivated a special connection with the story of Daniel in the lions' den, reading it through the lens of their own suffering. The African church told its story and recounted its theology visually through mosaics. A famous mosaic on display in the Bardo Museum in Tunis captures Daniel surrounded by lions. Like Daniel and his companions, these believers stood firm in their faith whether or not God chose to rescue them. Unlike Daniel, many North African believers witnessed for Christ as martyrs.

The most famous North African church martyrs were two young women (both nursing mothers) named Perpetua and Felicitas. Perpetua came from a prominent Carthaginian family, and Felicitas was her servant. Along with three brothers in the Lord, they were arrested for defying an imperial order against conversion to Christianity. At Perpetua's trial, even with her father's attempted intervention, she refused to renounce her faith and make a pagan sacrifice. She recorded in her diary:

> *Hilarianus the governor ... said to me: "Have pity on your father's gray head; have pity on your infant son. Offer the sacrifice for the welfare of the emperors."*
>
> *"I will not," I retorted.*
>
> *"Are you a Christian?" said Hilarianus.*
>
> *And I said: "Yes, I am." ...*
>
> *Then Hilarianus passed sentence on all of us: we were condemned to the beasts.*[22]

---

20 Irvin and Sunquist, *History of the World Christian Movement*, 26.
21 Decret, *Early Christianity in North Africa*, 10.
22 Musurillo, *Passion of Perpetua and Felicitas*, 2.2 in *Acts of the Christian Martyrs*.

Mauled by a mad red heifer and stabbed to death by Roman soldiers in the Carthage amphitheater, Perpetua and Felicitas died together as martyrs on March 7, 203.

Bold Witnesses

As many early-church believers went to trial for their Christian faith, they stood firm by refusing to deny their faith, affirming their identity as followers of Christ, and sharing the gospel. For some, their witness was a simple confession of being a Christian. In Polycarp of Smyrna's famous martyrdom account (d. 155), the bishop defended his refusal to make the pagan sacrifice by stating, "For eighty and six years I have been his servant, and he has done me no wrong, and how can I blaspheme my king who saved me?"[23]

During his trial, exile, and eventual execution in Carthage, Bishop Cyprian (d. 258) testified: "I am a Christian and a bishop. I recognize no other gods but the one true God who made heaven and earth, and the sea, and all that is in them."[24]

Justin Martyr responded to the Prefect Rusticus' interrogation by expanding further on the meaning of the gospel:

> *I have committed myself to the true doctrines of the Christians ... the belief that we piously hold regarding the God of the Christians, whom alone we hold to be the craftsman of the whole world from the beginning, and also regarding Jesus Christ, the child of God, who was foretold by the prophets as one who was to come down to mankind as a herald of salvation and teacher of good doctrines.*[25]

Speaking Truth to Power

Though Basil (329–379), the monk-bishop of Caesarea, did not die a martyr, he clashed significantly with the Roman Emperor Valens over theology. He held unswervingly to the Nicene Creed (that Christ and the Father share the same nature) against Valens' Arian leanings (that Christ was created by the Father). Though the emperor did not send Basil into exile, he divided Cappadocia in half, limiting Basil's influence over the churches and people in the region.

---

23 Musurillo, *Martyrdom of Polycarp*, 8–9.

24 Musurillo, *Acts of Cyprian*, 1, 3.

25 Musurillo, *Acts of Justin and Companions*, 2.

Basil's courage to speak truth to power comes through in his exchange with the Roman official Modestus, who threatened Bishop Basil because of his apparent lack of respect for both Emperor Valens and himself:

> *"Fear of what?" said Basil, "How could it affect me? ... Confiscation, banishment, torture, death. Have you no other threat?" said he, "for none of these can reach me." ... "Because ... a man who has nothing, is beyond the reach of confiscation; unless you demand my tattered rags, and the few books, which are my only possessions. Banishment is impossible for me, who am confined by no limit of place, counting my own neither the land where I now dwell, nor all of that into which I may be hurled. ... As for tortures, what hold can they have upon one whose body has ceased to be? ... Death is my benefactor, for it will send me the sooner to God."*
>
> *Amazed at this language, the prefect said, "No one has ever yet spoken thus, and with such boldness, to Modestus." "Why, perhaps," said Basil, "you have not met with a bishop ... where the interests of God are at stake, we care for nothing else, and make these our sole object."*[26]

During the Reformation in England, two martyrs—Hugh Latimer (1485–1555) and Nicholas Ridley (1500–1555)—defied both church and political authorities. Latimer served as the bishop of Worcester. An advocate for reading the Bible in English, he preached against the Catholic doctrine of purgatory and the use of icons in worship. When ordered by his bishop to denounce the teachings of Martin Luther (1483–1546), he refused, arguing that faith cannot be coerced by any form of earthly power. Latimer also preached against social injustices in English society. Ultimately, he resigned his post in opposition to Henry VIII's (r. 1509–1547) *Six Articles*, a treatise intended to make the English church more Roman Catholic.

Ridley served as a chaplain under Henry before becoming the bishop of London. Rejecting the Catholic transubstantiation view of the Eucharist (that the bread and wine literally become the body and blood of Christ), Ridley became increasingly convinced of Reformation ideas. He later assisted Archbishop Thomas Cranmer (1489–1556) in the development of *The Book of Common Prayer*, the definitive expression of Anglican theology and spirituality. On trial for heresy in 1555, Ridley was pressed by scholars from Oxford Divinity School over his views of papal authority. Ridley responded that Christ is the head of the church.

---

26 Gregory of Nazianzus, *Oration 43*, 49–50.

In 1553, the Catholic queen Mary Tudor (1516–1558) arrested Latimer, Ridley, and Cranmer and confined them to the Tower of London. Following their heresy trial in 1555, Latimer and Ridley were burned at the stake in Oxford. The following year, Cranmer suffered the same fate.[27]

One of the most famous martyrs of the twentieth century was Dietrich Bonhoeffer (1906–1945), a German Lutheran pastor who opposed the Nazi regime of Adolf Hitler (r. 1933–1945). As Hitler's power increased, many German Christians and churches accepted the führer's Aryan race (white supremacist) teachings. For Bonhoeffer, who had worshiped with African-American Christians in New York City and international believers in England and Spain, the church ceased to be the church when it embraced nationalism. He responded by helping launch the Confessing Church and affirming the Barmen Declaration, a statement that denounced Christian nationalism.[28] Bonhoeffer fully expected to suffer for these convictions.

> *And while I'm working with the church opposition with all my might, it's perfectly clear to me that this opposition is only a very temporary transitional phase on the way to an opposition of a very different kind, and that very few of those involved in this preliminary skirmish are going to be there for that second struggle. I believe that all of Christendom should be praying with us for the coming of resistance "to the point of shedding blood" and for the finding of people who can suffer it through.*[29]

Imprisoned for his opposition to the state in 1943, Bonhoeffer was implicated in the plot to kill Hitler, and on April 9, 1945, he was hanged. In a message to his friend, Bishop George Bell of Chichester, in what turned out to be his final words, Bonhoeffer wrote, "This is for me the end, but also the beginning. ... I believe in the principle of our universal Christian brotherhood which rises above all national hatreds and that our victory is certain."[30]

Bold Witness and Suffering in Contemporary Mission

Though the United Nations Declaration of Human Rights of 1948 contains an article on religious freedom, many nations continue to be intolerant

---

27 See further "Latimer, Hugh"; "Ridley, Nicholas"; "Cranmer, Thomas," *Oxford Dictionary of the Christian Church*.

28 See further Tietz, *Theologian of Resistance*, 40–49.

29 Cited in Tietz, 53.

30 Cited in Tietz, 110.

and even violent toward people of faith, including followers of Christ. While suffering for the gospel should never be romanticized, God still seems pleased to use suffering to allow his people a bold witness for Christ. We consider two twenty-first century examples.

Malatya Martyrs

On April 18, 2007, two Turkish pastors, Necati Ayden and Uğur Yuksel, and a German missionary, Tilmann Geske, welcomed five Turkish young men to an evangelistic Bible study. The pastors ran a Christian publishing house and led a small church in the southeastern Turkish city of Malatya. Posing as seekers with questions about the gospel, the five young men were actually part of a radical Islamic group. Once the Bible study began, they tied the pastors up, tortured them, and then slit their throats. They filmed the entire affair on their phones.

Aided by the media, news of the brutal massacre quickly spread throughout Turkey. Many Turkish Muslims were horrified by the murders, but they were also shocked by the response of the men's widows. When asked to comment about the events and the men who killed their husbands, the women declared that they chose to *forgive* them. Their message—a humble and bold witness for Christ—was also transmitted by the press all over Turkey. Though tragic, these men, their wives, and the Turkish church now had a witness on a scale they had not had before.[31]

Coptic Martyrs

On February 15, 2015, twenty Coptic Christians (plus one more from Ghana) were beheaded by members of ISIS on the beach in Sirte, Libya. The massacre was captured in a high-quality, five-minute short film which was then posted online. The Egyptian men were from a poor village in Upper Egypt and were working in Libya to send money home to their families. As Egyptian Christians, they followed the Coptic tradition, which they continued to practice during their time in Libya.

In the Coptic tradition, the entire liturgy is sung, and the choir assists the priest as worship leaders. Since some of these men had been trained as choir leaders, they would have known the entire liturgy by heart. With public worship opportunities limited in Libya, the men transformed their living space—one large room—into a worship area where they sang the liturgy, including prayers, hymns, and Scripture.

After being captured in January of 2015, the Christian brothers were tortured for forty-three days. Each day, they were ordered to say the Islamic

---
31 See further Wright, *Martyrs of Malatya*.

shahadah ("I declare there is no other god but Allah, and Muhammad is his messenger"), but they stood firm, refusing to deny their faith in Christ. Even amid beatings, the men continued to sing the liturgy and to worship.

One of the ISIS guards anonymously reported back to one of the men's family how impressed he was by their collective resolve to stand firm in their faith and to worship while being beaten. Just prior to their execution, the men were heard on film softly declaring in Arabic, "*Ya Rabbi Yessua* (O Lord Jesus)."[32] Though they experienced a brutal form of torture and execution, they boldly witnessed for Christ to their captors and to a watching world.

Summary: Bold Witness and Suffering in Mission Today

Following in the way of Daniel, many in Scripture and mission history have maintained a faithful witness despite enduring discrimination, hardship, and suffering. They testified to God's mighty acts and spoke truth to those in earthly places of authority without the expectation that God would rescue them from harm or even death. What does it mean to be a bold witness in the face of hardship today?

First, global Christians participating in God's mission must expect suffering. Many Western Christians were shocked in 2016 when American pastor Andrew Brunson was arrested and imprisoned in Turkey, having previously served in the country for over twenty years without incident. In the West, we are realizing that American and European citizens may no longer leverage the power that their passport countries once offered. Western Christians may face discrimination, intimidation, expulsion, or even imprisonment as global servants for Christ.

The majority world has much to teach the Western church about suffering. During the Iguassu Dialogue that met in Brazil in 1999, the assembled delegates, many of whom were Majority World Christian leaders, included this statement as part of their conference affirmation: "Suffering, persecution and martyrdom are present realities for many Christians. We acknowledge that our obedience in mission involves suffering and recognize that the church is experiencing this."[33] This captures a perspective on Christian suffering held by many Chinese, Indian, and Middle Eastern Christian workers serving in their own contexts. It also sheds light on the experience of Christian missionaries *from* Brazil,

---

32 See further Mosebach, *The 21*, 122–30.

33 Taylor, "Iguassu Affirmation," in *Global Missiology for the 21st Century*, 18.

Nigeria, and the Philippines laboring for the gospel in Muslim contexts like North Africa, the Middle East, and Central Asia. The majority-world church will continue to teach the global church about embracing suffering, resilience, and simple faith during persecution.

The church in Rwanda presents a winsome model for responding to hardship and suffering with a posture of mission. In a horrific display of tribalism during a one-hundred-day period in 1994, armed militias slaughtered nearly one million Rwandans. While the church of Rwanda has, of course, needed pastoral care and healing from this trauma, many church leaders are pursuing ministries of reconciliation among previously warring tribes and are also striving to plant new churches in Rwanda and in other countries.

Second, a bold witness amid suffering must always be a verbal witness. As Paul writes, "we preach Christ crucified" (1 Cor 1:23). Our good news is that Christ has suffered and died and risen. Those who respond in faith to the gospel have new life in Christ. Though Daniel and his companions witnessed through the integrity of their lives, they consistently opened their mouths and told the Babylonians and Persians who their God was. Even our most valiant humanitarian ministries will fall short of being Christian mission if we fail to proclaim Christ.

What does boldness in evangelism look like today? Is it the hellfire and brimstone preacher shouting on a street corner? Though I believe God can use all forms of witness, a bold witness is ideally located within personal relationships of friendship, trust, and hospitality. We ask questions and listen and strive to understand the worldview of our nonbelieving friends. We also proclaim our faith while demonstrating tangible acts of ministry, including caring for the physical and emotional needs of the poor and refugees.

But within those relationships, we also tell the truth to our friends: that we are sinners in need of a Savior, and that Savior is our Lord Jesus Christ. Missiologist Stephen Bevans refers to this as "prophetic dialogue."[34] Prophetic dialogue implies relationships, listening, and sharing the truth of the gospel—even when speaking up and sharing that truth is uncomfortable. Like a doctor who must give the bad news of a diagnosis before offering the good news of a treatment, we must share with other sinners how they can find forgiveness and a relationship with God.

---

34 Bevans, "Prophetic Dialogue Approach," 12.

Third, a bold witness will involve speaking truth to power in the public square. Like Dietrich Bonhoeffer, the church must continually rebuke Christian nationalism, especially as professing believers lose sight of the timeless principles of Scripture and conflate politics with faith. Following the spirit of the prophets of the Old Testament, we must denounce all forms of injustice: racism in all its forms; hate speech and crimes against particular cultural groups; and all forms of exploitation and corruption in the marketplace and in the political sphere.

Speaking truth to power also means advocating for those suffering for their faith in Christ. Embracing suffering does not contradict the global church's commitment to labor for justice. The Iguassu delegates add: "We affirm our privilege and responsibility to pray for those undergoing persecution. We are called to share in their pain, do what we can to relieve their sufferings, and work for human rights and religious freedom."[35]

Being a witness at work does not mean holding an evangelistic meeting or Bible study during work hours (though a Bible study before work or during lunch might be appropriate). Instead, we witness through our integrity and excellence on the job. Seeing work as worship, we carry out our tasks because we are doing it for the Lord. As coworkers observe our lives, we will have many opportunities to share the hope within us over a coffee break, lunch, or even by inviting a coworker home for a meal.

The workplace can often prove a hostile environment for followers of Christ. Christians will be pressured to compromise their integrity and engage in unethical behavior. While such a conflict may present opportunities to share a verbal witness, sometimes believers will need to resign before they compromise their integrity and witness.

Increasingly, Christians in the American university context face being "cancelled" because their commitment to historic Christian teaching conflicts with the university's values. Christians serving in politics may need to speak against corruption in that sphere, as well as warn against the tendency of some to embrace Christian nationalism. May we emulate Daniel and his companions to present a bold witness through a godly work ethic and the right words to accompany our actions.

---

35 Taylor, "Iguassu Affirmation," 18.

Questions for Reflection

1. Imagine if Daniel were your colleague at your place of work. What would his bold witness look like in your context?
2. What might hardship and suffering as a Christian look like in your place of work?
3. Not everyone has the temperament or spiritual gifts of Daniel or Dietrich Bonhoeffer. However, in what practical ways can a follower of Christ speak truth to power or denounce injustice in their social or political context?
4. After reading this chapter, what steps of faith do you need to take this week?

APPENDIX

Daniel: Background and Context

Daniel (ca. 620 BC–ca. 536 BC) lived during a tumultuous time in Israel's history.[1] A century before he was born, the Assyrians conquered the northern kingdom of Israel in 722 BC, forcing many Israelites into exile. In 612 BC, the Babylonians defeated the Assyrians, making them the dominant power in the ancient Near East for the better part of the next century. Part of that dominance included conquering Jerusalem and imposing exile on the inhabitants of Judah (the southern kingdom of Israel) in three waves: 605, 597, and 586 BC—the final conquest. During the first exile of 605 BC, Daniel and other privileged Jewish youth were forcibly displaced to Babylon and positioned in the service of the king.

The events in the book of Daniel begin with the reign of the Babylonian king, Nebuchadnezzar (605 BC), and continue through the third year of the Persian king, Cyrus the Great (536 BC), following the Persian conquest of the Babylonians in 539 BC. When the Persians came to power, they reversed the Babylonian policy and allowed the Judeans to return to

---

1 I am especially grateful to Old Testament scholars Brian Gault, Ben Noonan, and Bryan Beyer for offering some great feedback on this background appendix.

Jerusalem.² The book of Daniel ultimately highlights the rule of four great ancient empires—the Babylonians, Medo-Persians, Greeks, and Romans.³

When Jesus refers to the "abomination that causes desolation spoken of through the prophet Daniel" (Matt 24:15), he identifies Daniel as the author of the book.⁴ In at least two places within the text (Dan 9:2; 10:2), Daniel also claims authorship by referring to himself in the first person.⁵ Though we spend much time in this book meeting Daniel, for now we affirm that he was "a young man of noble blood who was exiled from Judah during the time of King Jehoiakim (609–597 BC) and lived thereafter at the Babylonian court. After the fall of the Babylonian Empire, he served the Medo-Persian Empire that succeeded it."⁶ An exile himself, Daniel was writing to other Jewish exiles living in Babylon. He most likely completed writing the book by the time of his death around 536 BC.⁷

Given the turbulent times that Daniel was living in, it's not surprising that the overarching theme of Daniel's book is "God's sovereignty over history and empires, setting up and removing kings as he pleases."⁸ Many commentators argue that the key verse of the book is Daniel 4:17: "The Most High is sovereign over all kingdoms of the earth."⁹ Since this theme is supported repeatedly in Daniel's narrative, Tremper Longman correctly notes that God's "sovereignty is not described abstractly in this book, but in the midst of the historical process, in the nitty-gritty of life."¹⁰

God's sovereignty over kings and nations points to the reality that God's kingdom is eternal and will never pass away. Several of Daniel's visions and dream interpretations highlight God's sovereign rule.¹¹ Though God's people will suffer hardship and exile in the present world, they are able to persevere and remain faithful in light of the future hope of God's kingdom. Speaking to the original Jewish audience as

---

2   See further Dan 1:1; 10:1; also Longman, *Daniel*, 21.
3   Some scholars do not include the Roman Empire. See further Longman, *Daniel*, 81.
4   In Matt 24:15, Jesus alludes to Dan 9:27, 11:31, and 12:11.
5   See further Archer and Youngblood, "Daniel: Introduction and Notes," 1459.
6   Duguid and Wegner, "Daniel: Introduction and Notes," 1581.
7   I hold to the traditional view that the book of Daniel was written in the sixth century and probably completed by 536 BC. See further Longman, *Daniel*, 22–24.
8   Duguid and Wegner, "Daniel: Introduction and Notes," 1582.
9   See further Archer and Youngblood, "Daniel: Introduction and Notes," 1460; also Fewell, *Circle of Sovereignty*, 12.
10 Longman, *Daniel*, 20. See further Dan 2:21; 4:34–37; 5:21.
11 See further Dan 7:11, 26–27; 8:25; 9:27.

well to pilgrims in a broken world today, "Daniel's main function is to reveal God to us."[12]

The Jewish Old Testament is divided into three portions of Scripture—the Torah (books of the Law), Prophets, and Writings (wisdom literature and historical books). In the Christian Old Testament canon, Daniel immediately follows the Major Prophets (Isaiah, Jeremiah, Ezekiel) but is listed as part of the Writings. Though Jesus refers to Daniel as a prophet and Daniel utters prophecies in the first person, he seems to lack the full status of a prophet. This could be because he lacks the sort of official call to being a prophet that characterize Isaiah, Jeremiah, and Ezekiel, or that, like Joseph and Esther, Daniel's primary place of service was in a foreign court outside of Israel.[13] Despite this, Daniel functions very much as a prophet.

When it comes to identifying genre, Daniel is divided evenly between historical narrative and apocalyptic literature. In the first six chapters of historical narrative (which do contain some visions that are apocalyptic in nature), we meet Daniel and his friends—Shadrach, Meshach, and Abednego—striving to honor God while living and working in a pagan court and society in Babylon.[14] The remaining chapters are apocalyptic: a

> *symbolic, visionary, prophetic literature, usually composed during oppressive conditions and being chiefly eschatological in theological content. Apocalyptic literature is primarily a literature of encouragement to the people of God.*[15]

Daniel prophesies about future events, such as the Maccabean revolt, the rise of the Roman Empire, and the reign of the Messiah.

In the present project, we focus primarily on the narrative chapters of Daniel, exploring the mission principles demonstrated in the life and ministry of Daniel, and to some extent, his companions. In the first chapter, we learn of Nebuchadnezzar's victory over Jehoiakim in Jerusalem, including the plunder of the articles from the temple that were taken to Babylon. Next, we learn that Daniel and a group of young Israelites are taken to Babylon to train for service in the court. Part of this training includes eating from the king's table. Not wanting to defile themselves, Daniel requests for himself and his friends a diet of vegetables and water,

---

12 Longman, *Daniel*, 20; see also Fewell, *Circle of Sovereignty*, 12.
13 See further Longman, *Daniel*, 22; Archer and Youngblood, "Daniel: Introduction and Notes," 1461.
14 See further Longman, *Daniel*, 28.
15 Archer and Youngblood, "Daniel: Introduction and Notes," 1460.

which renders them healthier and stronger than their peers. God blesses Daniel and his companions as they enter the king's service.

In the following chapter (Dan 2), we are introduced to one of Daniel's primary spiritual gifts—dream interpretation. King Nebuchadnezzar has a dream that no one in his court can interpret. In fact, the king wants the dream explained without having to recount it to anyone. Only Daniel, through God's power, is equal to the task. Because of Daniel's successful interpretation, Nebuchadnezzar promotes him and his friends to important administrative posts in the kingdom.

Next (Dan 3), Nebuchadnezzar crafts a gold image and orders everyone in Babylon to bow down to it. Thanks to some court officials who hated the Jews, Nebuchadnezzar learns that Shadrach, Meshach, and Abednego have refused to pay homage to the image. Furious at their disobedience, the king has the men thrown into a fiery furnace. But their bodies do not burn, and they are miraculously spared. Seeing this act of power, Nebuchadnezzar praises the God of Israel and promotes the men to even higher positions in the kingdom.

In the subsequent chapter (Dan 4), Daniel successfully interprets another of Nebuchadnezzar's dreams, one that precipitates the king suffering a period of insanity. When the king's sanity is restored, he responds by humbling himself and praising the God of heaven.

Later (Dan 5), King Belshazzar throws a banquet and uses the gold cups taken from the Jerusalem temple. Instead of worshiping the one true God, he offers praise to the gods of gold, silver, bronze, iron, wood, and stone. Because of this, Belshazzar literally sees writing on the wall, a message that he cannot understand. Called upon to interpret the message, Daniel announces the end of Belshazzar's reign, and by implication the end of his life, and the Medo-Persian conquest of the Babylonians.

In the final narrative chapter (Dan 6), some of the officials under the Persian King Darius convince the king to issue a temporary edict forbidding prayer to any god for the next thirty days, except to King Darius (Darius was likened to divinity). This was, of course, intended to entrap Daniel, who refuses to stop his habit of praying to the Lord openly three times a day. Because the edict was binding, Daniel is effectively sentenced to death by being thrown into a den of lions. Again, because of God's powerful protection, Daniel's life is spared.

This time, King Darius praises the God of Daniel; and "Daniel prospered during the reign of Darius and the reign of Cyrus the Persian" (Dan 6:28).[16]

---

16 Many commentators regard Darius and Cyrus as the same person.

Acknowledgments

Any project, such as writing a book, requires a village. My "village" includes friends who read this manuscript and offered valuable feedback. Brian Gault, Ben Noonan, Bryan Beyer, Robert Gallagher, and Abeneazer Urga spoke into this project from their respective areas of expertise (Old Testament studies, theology of mission, and New Testament studies).

I am also grateful for Ruth Buchanan, my writing coach and beta reader, who made great suggestions for making this book more inviting and readable.

I would like to give a shout-out to my theology of mission students at Columbia International University, who heard a good bit of this project "live" and (whether or not they liked it) provided an environment for me to work out my thoughts on Daniel and mission.

I am also thankful for my leadership at CIU, who celebrate writing and scholarship and allow that to be part of my job.

Finally, I would like to thank my wife, Shawn, who encourages me in the ministry of writing, and my kids—Brennan, Emma, and Eve—who think it's kind of cool that Dad writes books.

Bibliography

Archer, Gleason, and Ronald F. Youngblood. "Daniel: Introduction and Notes." In *NIV Study Bible*, edited by Kenneth L. Barker, 1459–86. Grand Rapids: Zondervan, 2020.

Ashford, Bruce Riley. *Every Square Inch: An Introduction to Cultural Engagement for Christians*. Bellingham: Lexham, 2015.

"BAM (Business as Mission) Global." https://bamglobal.org.

Basil. *Letters*. Volume 1 (1–185). Translated by Agnes Clare Way. Washington, DC: Catholic University Press, 1951.

Basil. *On the Holy Spirit*. Translated by David Anderson. Crestwood, NY: St. Vladimir's Seminary Press.

Baum, Wilhelm, and Dietmar W. Winkler. *The Church of the East: A Concise History*. London: Routledge, 2000.

Bede, Venerable. *Ecclesiastical History of the English People*. Edited by Judith McClure and Roger Collins. Oxford: Oxford University Press, 2009.

Bevans, Stephen. "A Prophetic Dialogue Approach." In *The Mission of the Church: Five Views in Conversation*, edited by Craig Ott. Grand Rapids: Baker Academic, 2016.

The Book of Common Prayer. Huntington Beach, CA: Anglican Liturgy Press, 2019.

Brother Andrew, *God's Smuggler*. Grand Rapids: Chosen, 2015.

"Cranmer, Thomas." *Oxford Dictionary of the Christian Church*. Edited by F. L. Cross and E. A. Livingstone. Oxford: Oxford University Press, 2005.

Cumming, Joseph. "Toward Respectful Witness." In *From Seed to Fruit: Global Trends, Fruitful Practices, and Emerging Issues among Muslims*, edited by J. Dudley Woodberry, 311–23. Pasadena: William Carey Library, 2008.

Davies, Oliver, and Thomas O'Loughin, eds. *Celtic Spirituality*. New York: Paulist, 1999.

Decret, François. *Early Christianity in North Africa*. Translated by Edward L. Smither. Eugene: Cascade, 2009.

Duguid, Iain M., and Paul D. Wegner. "Daniel: Introduction and Notes." In *ESV Study Bible*, edited by Lane T. Dennis et. al., 1581–1618. Wheaton: Crossway, 2008.

Elliot, Elisabeth. *Shadow of the Almighty: The Life and Testament of Jim Elliot.* New York: HarperCollins, 2009.

Elliot, Elisabeth. *Through Gates of Splendor.* Carol Stream: Tyndale, 1981.

"Every International." https://everyinternational.com.

Fernando, Ajith. *Spiritual Living in a Secular World: Applying the Book of Daniel Today.* Grand Rapids: Zondervan, 1993.

Fewell, Danna Nolan. *Circle of Sovereignty: Plotting Politics in the Book of Daniel.* Nashville: Abingdon, 1991.

"Figures at a Glance." *UNHCR: The UN Refugee Agency.* https://www.unhcr.org/en-us/figures-at-a-glance.html.

Flanders, Chris. "Vulnerable Mission" (editorial preface). *Missio Dei* 4:1 (February 2013). https://missiodeijournal.com/issues/md-4-1/authors/md-4-1-preface.

Glasser, Arthur. *Announcing the Kingdom: The Story of God's Mission in the Bible.* Grand Rapids: Baker Academic, 2003.

Goheen, Michael W., ed. *Reading the Bible Missionally.* Grand Rapids: Eerdmans, 2016.

Goldingay, John E. *Daniel: Word Biblical Commentary.* Dallas: Word, 1989.

Gregory of Nazianzus, *Oration 43, Nicene and Post-Nicene Fathers 2.7.* http://www.ccel.org/ccel/schaff/npnf207.iii.xxvi.html.

Gue, Patrick. "Toward a Haitian Wesleyan Contextual Theology." PhD diss., Columbia International University, 2020.

Hanciles, Jehu. *Migration and the Making of Global Christianity.* Grand Rapids: Eerdmans, 2021.

Harries, Jim. *Vulnerable Mission: Insights into Christian Mission to Africa from a Position of Vulnerability.* Pasadena: William Carey Library, 2011.

Hiebert, Paul G. "The Flaw of the Excluded Middle." *Missiology: An International Review* 10, no. 1 (1983): 146–58.

Hiebert, Paul G. "Power Encounter and Folk Islam." In *Muslims and Christians on the Emmaus Road,* edited by J. Dudley Woodberry, 54–60. Monrovia, CA: MARC, 1989.

"International Association for Refugees." https://www.iafr.org/learn.

Irvin, Dale T., and Scott W. Sunquist. *History of the World Christian Movement: Volume I, Earliest Christianity to 1453.* Maryknoll, NY: Orbis, 2004.

Israel, Emma, and Jeanne Batalova. "International Students in the United States." *Migration Policy Institute.* https://www.migrationpolicy.org/article/international-students-united-states-2020.

Jipp, Joshua. *Saved by Faith and Hospitality*. Grand Rapids: Eerdmans, 2017.

"Jonathan House." https://www.iafr.org/project/jonathan-house.

Kerr, David A. "Cragg, Albert Kenneth." In *Biographical Dictionary of Christian Missions*, edited by Gerald H. Anderson. https://www.bu.edu/missiology/missionary-biography/c-d/cragg-albert-kenneth-1913/.

Kraft, Charles. "What Kind of Encounters Do We Need in Our Christian Witness?" *Evangelical Missions Quarterly* 27, no. 3 (1991): 258–67.

Lai, Patrick. *Business for Transformation: Getting Started*. Pasadena: William Carey Library, 2015.

Lai, Patrick. *Tentmaking: The Life and Work of Business as Missions*. Colorado Springs: Authentic, 2005.

"Latimer, Hugh." *Oxford Dictionary of the Christian Church*. Edited by F. L. Cross and E. A. Livingstone. Oxford: Oxford University Press, 2005.

Leithart, Peter J. *Baptism: A Guide from Life to Death*. Bellingham, WA: Lexham, 2021.

Liefield, Olive Fleming. *Unfolding Destinies: The Unfolding Story of the Auca Mission*. Grand Rapids: Discovery House, 1998.

Longman, Tremper. *Daniel: The NIV Application Commentary*. Grand Rapids: Zondervan, 1999.

Love, Rick. *Muslims, Magic, and the Kingdom of God*. Pasadena: William Carey Library, 2000.

McNeill, John T. *The Celtic Churches: A History A.D. 200–1200*. Chicago: University of Chicago Press, 1974.

Mosebach, Martin. *The 21: A Journey into the Land of Coptic Martyrs*. Walden, NY: Plough, 2019.

Mouw, Richard J. *Abraham Kuyper: A Short and Personal Introduction*. Grand Rapids: Eerdmans, 2011.

Musurillo, Herbert, ed., *Acts of the Christian Martyrs*. Oxford: Oxford University Press, 1999.

Myers, Bryant L. *Engaging Globalization: The Poor, Christian Mission, and Our Hyperconnected World*. Grand Rapids: Baker Academic, 2017.

O'Loughlin, Thomas. *St. Patrick: The Man and His Works*. London: SPCK, 1999.

Packer, J. I. *Knowing God*. Downers Grove: IVP, 1973.

"Persons of Peace." International Mission Board, *IMB Topics*. https://www.imb.org/topic-term/persons-of-peace/.

Plummer, Jo. "What Is Business as Mission?" *The BAM Review* blog, January 14, 2015. https://businessasmission.com/what-is-bam/.

"The Refugee Highway." https://bit.ly/3Pf6mbV.

"Ridley, Nicholas." *Oxford Dictionary of the Christian Church*. Edited by F. L. Cross and E. A. Livingstone. Oxford: Oxford University Press, 2005.

Robert, Dana. *Christian Mission: How Christianity Became a World Religion*. Hoboken: Wiley-Blackwell, 2009.

"The Seoul Declaration on Diaspora Missiology." Lausanne Movement. November 14, 2009. https://lausanne.org/content/statement/the-seoul-declaration-on-diaspora-missiology.

Shenk, David. "The Legacy of William Wadé Harris." *International Bulletin of Missionary Research* 10, no. 4 (October 1986): 170–76.

Smither, Edward L. *Augustine as Mentor: A Model for Preparing Spiritual Leaders*. Nashville: B&H Academic, 2008.

Smither, Edward L. *Christian Martyrdom: A Brief History with Reflections for Today*. Eugene: Cascade, 2020.

Smither, Edward L. *Mission as Hospitality: Imitating the Hospitable God in Mission*. Eugene: Cascade, 2021.

Smither, Edward L. *Missionary Monks: An Introduction to the History and Theology of Missionary Monasticism*. Eugene: Cascade, 2016.

Smither, Edward L., and Trevor Castor. "Timothy I of Baghdad: A Model for Peaceful Dialogue." In *The History of Apologetics: A Biographical and Methodological Introduction*, edited by Benjamin Forrest et al., 197–209. Grand Rapids: Zondervan, 2020.

Steger, Manfred. *Globalization: A Very Short Introduction*. Oxford: Oxford University Press, 2020.

Sunquist, Scott W. *Understanding Christian Mission: Participation in Suffering and Glory*. Grand Rapids: Baker Academic, 2013.

Talbot, C. H. *The Life of Boniface. Internet Medieval Sourcebook*, Fordham University. https://sourcebooks.fordham.edu/basis/willibald-boniface.asp.

Taylor, William D., ed. *Global Missiology for the 21st Century: The Iguassu Dialogue*. Grand Rapids: Baker Academic, 2000.

Tietz, Christiane. *Theologian of Resistance: The Life and Thoughts of Dietrich Bonhoeffer*. Translated by Victoria J. Barnett. Minneapolis: Fortress, 2016.

Wagenman, Michael R. *Engaging the World with Abraham Kuyper*. Bellingham, WA: Lexham, 2019.

Walls, Andrew F. "Toward a Theology of Migration." In *Crossing Cultural Frontiers: Studies in the History of World Christianity*, edited by Mark R. Gornick, 49–61. Maryknoll, NY: Orbis, 2017.

Watson, David L., and Paul D. Watson. *Contagious Disciple Making: Leading Others on a Journey of Discovery*. Nashville: Thomas Nelson, 2014.

Wilken, Robert. *The First Thousand Years: A Global History of Christianity*. New Haven: Yale University Press, 2013.

"William Wilberforce: Antislavery Politician." *Christian History*. https://www.christianitytoday.com/history/people/activists/william-wilberforce.html.

"The Willowbank Report: Consultation on Gospel and Culture." *Lausanne Occasional Paper 2*. 1978. http://www.lausanne.org/all-documents/lop-2.html#1.

Wilson, J. Christy. *Today's Tentmakers: Self-Support: An Alternative Model for Worldwide Witness*. Eugene: Wipf & Stock, 2002.

Wright, Christopher J. H. *The Mission of God: Unlocking the Bible's Grand Narrative*. Downers Grove: IVP Academic, 2006.

Wright, Christopher J. H. "A Shared Human Condition: An Old Testament Refugee Perspective." In *Refugee Diaspora: Missions Amid the Greatest Humanitarian Crisis of Our Times*, edited by Sam George and Miriam Adeney, 143–52. Pasadena: William Carey Library, 2018.

Wright, James. *Martyrs of Malatya: Martyred for the Messiah in Turkey*. Welwyn Garden City, UK: Evangelical Press, 2015.

Yeh, Allen. *Polycentric Missiology: 21st Century Mission from Everywhere to Everyone*. Downers Grove: IVP Academic, 2016.

Scripture Index

Genesis
1:28   3, 29
3:4–19   3
11:1–9   4
12:1–3   7
26:2–5   4
32:22–32   4
37:18–36   4
39:2–4   35
39:4   20
39:20–21   36
39:22   20
41:1–41   36
41:41   20
41:46–57   20

Exodus
6:7   56
12:1–30   56
12:38   56
15:11   57
15:15   56
20:3–4   73
22:21   8
31:2–11   21

Leviticus
11:1–47   16
19:33–34   8

Deuteronomy
4:27   5
14:3–20   16
32:8–9   7

Joshua
2:9–11   56
5:13–6:27   57

Judges
3:7   21
4:5   21
5:31   21

Ruth
2:1–4:13   8

1 Samuel
13:14   21
17:45   57
17:46   57
18:5   22
18:12–16   22

2 Samuel
14:25   16

1 Kings
3:5   22
3:7, 9   22
3:13   22
3:16–28   22
4:30–34   22
10:1–13   23

2 Kings
5:15   57

Nehemiah
1:11   36
2:3   23, 36
2:4–9   36
2:6–9   23
2:19–20   23
4:1–23   23
5:1–19   23
6:1–19   23
10:1   23
13:1–31   23

Esther
2:5–10   36
2:8–9   36
2:17   37
2:21–23   37
5:3   37
7:3–4   37
9:29–10:3   37

MISSION IN THE WAY OF DANIEL

Psalms

2:10–11 58
22:27–28 57
34:7 53
55:17 74
78 57
78:13 57
78:43 57
78:55 57
86:8 58
96:3 ix
96:5 58
105 57
106 57

Isaiah

40:3–5 78
47 18
52:13–53:12 79

Jeremiah

29:7 19

Daniel

1:2 5
1:3–5 16
1:4 17
1:8–10 32
1:8–16 16
1:11–16 32
1:17 2, 18
1:17–20 16
1:20 18
1:21 2
2:1–11 33
2:11 48
2:12 33
2:14 33
2:14b–15 33
2:16 33
2:17–18 48
2:18 74
2:19 48
2:20–23 49
2:25 71
2:27–28 72
2:37 72
2:44–45 49, 75
2:45 72
2:46–49 33
2:47 76
2:48 18
2:49 18
3:8–12 71
3:12 3, 71
3:15 73
3:18 74
3:25 53
3:26 53
3:27 53
3:28 53
3:28–29 77
3:29 34, 54
3:30 18
4:1 76
4:2–3 50, 76
4:8–9 55
4:9 49
4:17 55, 92
4:25 73
4:30 50
4:34–35 51, 76, 77
5:5 51
5:11 52, 55
5:13 71
5:14 55
5:18 52
5:21 52
5:23 73
5:26 52
5:27 73
5:30–31 19
6:6–7 54
6:10 74
6:13 19, 71, 74
6:16 34, 54
6:22 54
6:24 34
6:25 77
6:26–27 54
6:28 35, 94
7:13–14 75
9:2 92
9:3 74
9:4–11 6
9:26 75
10:1–21 74
10:2 92
10:13 55

Scripture Index

Matthew
2:13–18   4
5:13–14   29
11:12   79
24:14   10
28:18–20   ix, 10

Mark
5:2   58
5:20   59
6:17–29   79

Luke
3:4   78
3:19–20   78
4:18–19   59
4:28–29   79
10:5–6   38
18:41–43   58

John
2:1–11   58
2:11   58
5:8   58

Acts
1:8   4
2:2–4   59
2:5   7
2:6–11   7
2:9   14
2:37–38   60
2:41   8, 60
5:12–42   80
5:29   40, 80
5:38–39   38
8:1   4
9:16   80
16:16–40   60
28:2   39
28:7–10   39

Romans
1:4   59

1 Corinthians
1:23   87

2 Corinthians
1:5   80
11:23–26   80
12:10   80

Galatians
3:8   7
6:17   80

Ephesians
6:12–13   60

Philippians
2:6   79

Colossians
1:24   80
2:15   59

1 Peter
1:1–2   9
2:4–8a   75
2:12   9

Topical Index

A

Abednego 2–3, 18–19, 32–34, 48, 50, 53, 55, 73–74, 77, 94
Abraham 4, 7
Abrahamic pattern 10, 13
Adam 3
Agathangelos (Armenian historian) 61
ancient Near East 57
Arafat, Yassar 42
Artaxerxes, King 23, 36
Ashpenaz (Babylonian court official) 1, 15, 31–32
Assyrians 5, 91
asylum seekers x, 11, 13
Augustine of Canterbury 40
Augustine, Saint 44
Ayden, Necati 85

B

Babel 7
Babylon 1–2, 14–15, 19, 29, 31, 33, 50
Babylonian
    court 2, 17
    deities 2
    Empire 92
    language 17
    literature 17
    polytheism 73
    sages 33, 52
    thinking 18

Babylonians ix, 2–3, 5, 8, 17–18, 26, 71, 73, 87, 91, 94
Baghdad 41, 43
Basil (monk-bishop) 82–83
Belshazzar, King 18, 51–52, 73, 94
Bevans, Stephen 87
Bonhoeffer, Dietrich 84, 88
Boniface (monk) 62
British Isles 40
Brother Andrew 42
Brunson, Andrew 86
Buddhism 41
Bush, George H. W. 43
business as mission (BAM) 27

C

cancelled 88
Canterbury 40
Cappadocia 82
Carthage 82
Celtic Christians 69
China x, 24–25, 41
Church of the East 24, 41
Columba (Irish monk) 40, 44
Cragg, Kenneth 26
Cranmer, Thomas 83
Cumming, Joseph 42
Cyprian, Bishop 82
Cyrus, King 2, 35

Topical Index

D

Darius the Mede 19, 34–35, 52, 54–55, 74, 77–78, 94
David, King 17, 21–22
Deborah 21
diaspora
 Jews 36
 missiology 12
 missionary 14
 world ix, 12–13
displaced x, 1, 8–14, 18, 31, 91
displacement 3, 5, 11
dream interpretation 19
dream(s) 33, 48–50, 52, 55, 94

E

Ecuador 63
Egypt 4–5, 20
Egyptian(s) 20, 56, 85
Elliot, Jim 63
Esther 36–37
exiles, Jewish 2, 16–17, 23, 35, 52, 71–72, 92
Exodus 4, 51, 56

F

favor x, 31–32, 35–37, 41–45
Felicitas 81–82
Fernando, Ajith 18
fiery furnace 18, 34, 50, 52, 55, 71, 73, 77, 94
first-century church 79
first dream of Nebuchadnezzar 33, 48–49, 72, 74–76
Fleming, Pete 63

folk religion 48, 65
foreigner(s) 2, 6, 8

G

Genghis Khan 41
Geske, Tilmann 85
globalization 10–11
God's Smuggler 42
Goldingay, John 5–6, 58
gold statue 52, 73, 94
government
 administrators 23, 73
 officials 30, 42
 positions 28
 posts 19
 service 71
Great Britain 26
Gregory of Rome, Bishop 40
Gregory the Illuminator 61

H

Harris, William Wadé 63
Herod 78
Hezbollah 42–43
Hiebert, Paul 65
Holy Spirit 7, 14, 59–60, 63, 68
Hussein, Saddam 43

I

Iguassu Dialogue 86, 88
immigrant(s) 11, 13
immigration 11
international students 11–13

I

Ireland 10
Irish 9–10
ISIS 86
Islam 24, 41, 43
Islam, folk 65
Israel 3, 5, 8, 18, 21–22, 56
Israelites 1–2, 15, 21, 36, 56

J

Jacob 4
Jerusalem 5, 14, 23, 26, 31, 36, 91
John of Montecorvino (Franciscan) 41
John the Baptizer 78–79
Joseph 4–5, 8, 10, 20, 35–36
Justin Martyr 82

K

Kantor, Rosabeth Moss 10
Kraft, Charles 67
Kuyper, Abraham 29

L

Latimer, Hugh 83
Latin America 28, 45, 67
leaders
    Muslim 41–42
    political ix, x, 44–45, 47, 55
    religious 38, 58, 79, 87
    skilled 19
leadership 2, 18–21, 23, 35, 37, 45
Liberia 63
Libya 85
lions' den 19, 34, 54, 72, 75, 77, 94
Love, Rick 66
Luther, Martin 83

M

Mahdi (Muslim Caliph) 41
marketplace x, xi, 29
martyrdom 64, 82
martyrs 24, 73, 81–82, 84–85
massacre 85
Matteo Ricci 24
McCully, Ed 63
Medo-Persian Empire 52, 92
Meshach 2–3, 18–19, 32–34, 48, 50, 53, 55, 73–74, 77, 94
Middle East 28, 47, 64, 86
migration 3, 5–6, 9, 11–13
mission ix, xi, 12, 29
    African 63
    contexts 28
    hermeneutic xi
    history x, xi, 9, 13, 24, 39, 44, 61–62, 86
    in Scripture 20, 35, 56, 78
    of God xi, 6, 12–13, 23, 39
    Old Testament 23
    power 67
    practice 10
missionary monks 39
monasteries 10, 24
Mongol Empire 41
monks 24, 40
Moses 20–21

Topical Index

Mubarak, Hosni   43
Muhammad, Prophet   41, 86
Muslims   x, 26, 28, 42, 65
Muslims, folk   66

N

Nebuchadnezzar, King   1, 3, 5–6, 31–34, 48–50, 52–53, 55, 72–73, 75–76, 94
Nehemiah   23, 36
Nicene Creed   82
Nicolas IV, Pope   41
North Africa   87
North African Church   81

O

Open Doors   42

P

Patrick of Ireland   9–10, 39, 44
Paul, Apostle   39, 60, 80
peace   71
people of peace   38–39, 45
Perpetua   81–82
Persia   2, 14–15, 19, 24, 29, 31, 41
Persian Empire   19, 24, 38
Persians   ix, 2, 8, 38, 87
Pharaoh   20, 36, 56
Polycarp of Smyrna   82
power   x, 18, 47–52, 54–57, 59, 64, 69, 73, 88, 94
power encounter(s)   58, 61–64, 67
power in mission   xi
prayer, intercessory   55

R

refugee highway   12–13
refugee(s)   x, 11–13, 29, 47, 79, 81, 87
Ridley, Nicholas   83
Rwanda   87

S

Saint, Nate   63
second dream of Nebuchadnezzar   72, 76
Shadrach   2–3, 18–19, 32–34, 48, 50, 53, 55, 73–74, 77, 94
shahadah   86
Silas   60
skills, natural   ix, x, 15, 17, 35
skills, professional   ix, x, 13, 25, 27, 29
Solomon, King   17, 22
spiritual warfare   55, 60, 66–69, 74
stranger(s)   6, 8
suffering   ix, xi, 42–43, 68, 71–72, 78–80, 85–88
Suffering Servant   79

T

tentmaking   26
The Passion of the Christ   43
Timothy of Baghdad   41
Tower of Babel   3, 6, 60
Turkey   85

U

United Nations Declaration of Human Rights   84

V

Valens, Emperor   82
visions   9–10, 16, 18, 74, 92–93
vulnerability   x, 13–14
vulnerable   1, 8–9

W

Walls, Andrew   3
Waodoni   63
West Africans   63
Wilberforce, William   25–26
Woodberry, Dudley   65
Wright, Christopher   3

X

Xerxes, King   36–37

Y

Youderian, Roger   63
Yuksel, Uğur   85

Other books that may interest you —available @ missionbooks.org

Ephesiology
A Study of the Ephesian Movement
Michael T. Cooper (Author)

Ephesiology offers a comprehensive view of the redemptive movement of the Holy Spirit in this city and compels us to ask the question: how can we effectively connect Christ to our culture? Through this study of a movement, discover how the Holy-Spirit still changes lives, cities, and the world.

234-page Paperback: $15.99
eBook: $9.99

Controversies in Mission
Theology, People, and Practice of Mission in the 21st Century [EMS 24]
Rochelle Cathcart Scheuermann, Edward L. Smither (Editors)

Crossing social, cultural, and religious barriers and making disciples of all nations has probably never been without some level of controversy. This book is an attempt to hit the pause button on this rapid-paced world and to reflect on how we do mission, especially in light of the new layers of complexity that globalization brings.

338-page Paperback: $19.99
eBook: $9.99

Mobilizing Gen Z

Challenges and Opportunities for the Global Age of Missions

Jolene Erlacher & Katy White (Authors)

In *Mobilizing Gen Z*, Jolene Erlacher and Katy White blend leading research with the voices of current mission practitioners to unpack the dynamics behind our changing culture and the resulting impact on the church. And perhaps not-so-surprisingly, they reach the conclusion that God has already provided a solution for such a time as this—Gen Z (b. 1996-2010).

194-page Paperback: $14.99
eBook: $9.99

Learning to Lead at the Feet of Jesus

Encounters with Grace and Truth

Todd Poulter (Author)

Poulter draws on a wide variety of cross-cultural experiences and invites leaders to a refreshing journey of discovery, intimacy, and transformation. With reflective questions designed to provoke insight and self-awareness, this book challenges readers to deepen their understanding and appreciation of Jesus, and evaluate their own beliefs, assumptions, and cultural expectations about leadership.

208-page Paperback: $15.99
eBook: $9.99

www.ingramcontent.com/pod-product-compliance
Lightning Source LLC
Chambersburg PA
CBHW071248070526
44583CB00017B/2381